PAUL OF ARABIA

PAUL OF ARABIA

The Hidden Years of the Apostle to the Gentiles

by
BEN WITHERINGTON III
& JASON A. MYERS

CASCADE *Books* • Eugene, Oregon

PAUL OF ARABIA
The Hidden Years of the Apostle to the Gentiles

Copyright © 2020 Ben Witherington III and Jason A. Myers. All rights reserved. Except for brief quotations in critical publications or reviews, no part of this book may be reproduced in any manner without prior written permission from the publisher. Write: Permissions, Wipf and Stock Publishers, 199 W. 8th Ave., Suite 3, Eugene, OR 97401.

Cascade Books
An Imprint of Wipf and Stock Publishers
199 W. 8th Ave., Suite 3
Eugene, OR 97401

www.wipfandstock.com

PAPERBACK ISBN: 978-1-5326-9822-4
HARDCOVER ISBN: 978-1-5326-9823-1
EBOOK ISBN: 978-1-5326-9824-8

Cataloguing-in-Publication data:

Names: Witherington, Ben, III, author | Myers, Jason A., author
Title: Paul of Arabia : the hidden years of the apostle to the Gentiles / by Ben Witherington III and Jason A. Myers.
Description: Eugene, OR: Cascade Books, 2020 | Includes bibliographical references.
Identifiers: ISBN 978-1-5326-9822-4 (paperback) | ISBN 978-1-5326-9823-1 (hardcover) | ISBN 978-1-5326-9824-8 (ebook)
Subjects: LCSH: Paul, the Apostle, Saint. | Apostles—Biography.
Classification: BS2506 W58 2020 (print) | BS2506 (ebook)

Manufactured in the U.S.A.   MARCH 26, 2025

To the camel drivers of Petra, who kept me entertained. Next time I want to ride the one you called Michael Jackson, should be a thriller.
—Ben Witherington

To Lisa and Augustine Matthew, forever my loves.
—Jason A. Myers

Contents

Preface | xi
Acknowledgments | xiii
Abbreviations | xiv

Chapter One: **Desert Storm** | 1

Chapter Two: **The Nomadic Nabateans** | 10

Chapter Three: **Aliens and Allies, Slaves and Thieves** | 21

Chapter Four: **Arrival at the Rose City** | 27

Chapter Five: **Solitary Saul** | 36

Chapter Six: **The Love of Labor** | 40

Chapter Seven: **News From Judaea** | 46

Chapter Eight: **Trouble in Zion** | 54

Chapter Nine: **Festival Time** | 59

Chapter Ten: **The Jewels of Petra** | 66

Chapter Eleven: **The King's Speech** | 69

Chapter Twelve: **The Quickening** | 74

Chapter Thirteen: **The Journey to Aela** | 85

Chapter Fourteen: **The Spy** | 89

Chapter Fifteen: **A Close Shave on the Wedding Day** | 91

Chapter Sixteen: **Marital Bliss** | 97

Chapter Seventeen: **Planning the Journey to Jebel Musa** | 99

Chapter Eighteen: **Wafi in the Lead** | 102

Chapter Nineteen: **Sailing South** | 106

Chapter Twenty: **A Long Day's Journey into Night** | 108

Chapter Twenty-One: **The Mountain of Moses** | 111

Chapter Twenty-Two: **The Return to the Sea** | 114

Chapter Twenty-Three: **Domestic Fertility or Futility?** | 116

Chapter Twenty-Four: **A Day of Dread** | 124

Chapter Twenty-Five: **A Winter of Disease and Discontent** | 130

Chapter Twenty-Six: **Back to Damascus** | 135

Chapter Twenty-Seven: **The "Rock" Meets the Man from Rock City** | 139

Chapter Twenty-Eight: **Return to Cilicia** | 143

Chapter Twenty-Nine: **The Synagogue Sermon** | 150

Chapter Thirty: **Antioch on the Orontes** | 153

Chapter Thirty-One: **The Second Return to Zion** | 158

Chapter Thirty-Two: **The Secret Meeting** | 161

Chapter Thirty-Three: **Saul and Barnabas Apostles: from Antioch** | 166

Chapter Thirty-Four: **Return to Antioch** | 170

Postscript | 175
Bibliography | 176

From Wikipedia we learn: "In October 1917, as part of a general effort to divert Ottoman military resources away from the British advance before the Third battle of Gaza, a revolt of Arabs in Petra was led by British Army officer T. E. Lawrence (Lawrence of Arabia) against the Ottoman regime. The Bedouin women living in the vicinity of Petra and under the leadership of Sheik Khallil's wife were gathered to fight in the revolt of the city. The rebellions, with the support of British military, were able to devastate the Ottoman forces." (https://en.wikipedia.org/wiki/Petra, accessed 12-12-18)

In Paul's second letter to the church in Corinth we read: "In Damascus the governor under King Aretas had the city of the Damascenes guarded in order to arrest me. But I was lowered in a basket from a window in the wall and slipped through his hands . . . I know a man in Christ who fourteen years ago was caught up to the third heaven. Whether it was in the body or out of the body I do not know—God knows. And I know that this man—whether in the body or apart from the body I do not know, but God knows— was caught up to paradise and heard inexpressible things, things that no one is permitted to tell. I will boast about a man like that, but I will not boast about myself, except about my weaknesses. Even if I should choose to boast, I would not be a fool, because I would be speaking the truth. But I refrain, so no one will think more of me than is warranted by what I do or say, or because of these surpassingly great revelations. Therefore, in order to keep me from becoming conceited, I was given a thorn in my flesh, a messenger of Satan, to torment me. Three times I pleaded with the Lord to take it away from me. But he said to me, 'My grace is sufficient for you, for my power is made perfect in weakness.' Therefore, I will boast all the more gladly about my weaknesses, so that Christ's power may rest on me. That is why, for Christ's sake, I delight in weaknesses, in insults, in hardships, in persecutions, in difficulties. For when I am weak, then I am strong." (2 Cor. 11:32—12:10)

PREFACE

FIGURING OUT WHAT HAPPENED TO SAUL OF TARSUS BETWEEN THE TIME he had his Damascus Road experience and the time he resurfaces as a missionary sent by the church at Antioch with Barnabas to evangelize Cyprus is notoriously difficult. For one thing, so far as we can tell, Paul wrote no letters to converts before he actually had converts, which is to say only after his mission in Galatia. But this is at a minimum some fourteen years into his Christian life! What was he doing all those years before "the first missionary journey" to the west of Antioch? There have been very few helpful scholarly studies on this portion of Paul's life, but two are worthy of mention—R. Riesner's *Paul's Early Period* (Westminster John Knox, 1998), and before that M. Hengel's and A.M. Schwemer's, *Paul between Damascus and Antioch: The Unknown Years* (Eerdmans, 1997).

A further difficulty is that Luke's Acts is precious little help because: 1) *he never mentions Paul's missionary letters*, concentrating instead on his oral proclamation as an evangelist; 2) he skims over the early period between Paul's time in Damascus and when he is brought from Tarsus to Antioch by Barnabas. So we have to rely on hints and clues from Paul's earliest letters, particularly Galatians and 1 and 2 Corinthians. I believe there are just enough clues in these letters to piece together a reasonable portrait of Paul's early years as a follower of Christ. What follows in this historical novel of course involves a good deal of filling in the gaps by means of creative thinking and imagination, but even when I am most speculative there is some basis in Paul's letters or Acts for such a thought experiment.

To give but one example, is there a reason to think Paul may have been married at some juncture? There are several good reasons to think so: 1) Saul of Tarsus was converted after he had already been advancing in Judaism, and was a notable Pharisee. Jews normally married before the age Saul had reached when he had his Damascus road experience; 2) there are other small hints, for example in 1 Cor 7, Paul seems to show some real understanding of what widows or widowers go through and he does not oppose their remarriage, "only marry in the Lord." This has suggested to some scholars that Paul must have been married and lost his spouse at some juncture; 3) there is the further little hint in 1 Cor 9:5, Paul asks rhetorically—"don't I have the right to have (and travel with) a Christian sister as a wife like the other apostles?" The implied answer is yes, though by the time he writes 1 Corinthians he does not have a wife. But why even mention this if Paul had never been married? After all, he had finished talking about marriage in 1 Cor 7, and in 1 Cor 9 he is talking about rights that he has *given up*. I could say a good deal more, but I will let the novel speak for itself. I hope you enjoy this thought experiment as much as I enjoyed creating it.

As the old adage goes: "the past is like a foreign country, they do things differently there." Such a motto is the inspiration for the closer look sections placed strategically throughout the book. These sections are the form of an ancient tour guide, helping to illumine and explain various cultural elements of the ancient world. While there are some aspects that unite humans across space and time, there's a lot that changes from time to time and from culture to culture. We are meaning-seeking creatures and as such our brains often fill in the gaps of what we don't know based on our own experience. Sometimes this is helpful, sometimes, unhelpful. The closer look sections hope to spark a interest in the various cultural background issues that aid the story and help readers close the gap between ancient and modern worlds! As for the division of labor, Ben wrote the narrative chapters, while Jason wrote the closer look sections.

—Ben Witherington and Jason A. Myers

EASTER 2019

ACKNOWLEDGMENTS

I am very happy to see this work come to fruition. Thanks to Jason Myers for all his hard work on this project and writing the closer look sections to engage readers in the world of the New Testament. Many thanks to our mutual friend, Michael Thomson, for pursuing this project and seeing what it could become.

—Ben Witherington

My love and interest of ancient history was spurred on by my teachers. Both Ben Witherington and Craig Keener, my doctoral supervisors, instilled in me a love for social world of the New Testament. This work is a testament to their influence on my own work and for which I owe them greatly.

To my wife, Lisa, and my son, Augustine Matthew. Their support over the project was without end. Allowing me to travel and do research, to spend extra time in the office, only helped to make this project what it became. There's no way I could do the work I get to do without them.

A great appreciation is extended to the warm fellowship and great resources of Tyndale House in Cambridge, England. The treasure of Tyndale allowed me the privilege of writing some of the closer look sections in an ever efficient way.

—Jason A. Myers

ABBREVIATIONS

OCD   *Oxford Classical Dictionary*, 3rd edition. Simon Hornblower and Antony Spawforth, eds. New York: Oxford University Press, 1999.

NTPG   N. T. Wright. *The New Testament and the People of God*. Christian Origins and the Question of God, vol. 1. Minneapolis: Fortress, 1992.

CHAPTER ONE

DESERT STORM

The journey to Petra was long, exceedingly long, some 300 Roman miles or more.[1] Even under good conditions the journey would take at least ten days from Damascus, but only twenty miles out of Damascus, Saul and his lone companion and guide for the journey, Abram, had run into a *hamsin*, a desert storm. It was severe enough to impede travel, but not severe enough to make Saul want to stop the journey, which left Abram muttering and cursing and the donkey he was pulling along braying and resisting going forward. Fortunately, they were on the major north-south road, the spice road, so there were plenty of travelers going in both directions, despite the storm. There is something to be said for safety in numbers, and fortunately Abram knew of a *caravanserai* only five or so miles further south where they could put up for the night. They had already passed one camel caravan heading north, the animals loaded down with large amphorae of oil and spices of various sorts. Wrapping his mantle around his face, Abram doggedly pushed forward, the sand stinging his eyes. Saul said nothing, simply leaning into the prevailing wind and kept pressing inexorably forward. He had left Damascus in a hurry, before the Sanhedrin's "investigators" had arrived to query why he had not returned to Jerusalem with captured Christ-followers, as he had promised when he left Mt. Zion. He was a man on the run. He was also a man without a people. The Sanhedrin wanted him in the worst way, and the Christ-followers in Judea were scared to death of him.

---

1. A Roman mile was 5,000 feet long, whereas the current British/American mile is 5,280 feet.

Yet he was also a man on a mission. He did not want to be disobedient to the heavenly vision, which had commissioned him to go and proclaim to those who were not Jews the message about Jesus being not only the Jewish messiah but also a light to the nations. None of his companions who had traveled with him from Jerusalem to Damascus had had the vision and the specific communication from the heavenly voice, but they had seen a light and heard a sound and knew something odd was happening to Saul of Tarsus, not least when they saw the scales on his eyes and had to lead him by the hand into Damascus. They understandably assumed he had been cursed by God (since blinding was a known punishment for sin),[2] and they were all too happy to abandon him to his fate in Damascus, once they left him at a Jewish hostel there.

"Thank God for Ananias," said Saul days later when he was visited by that frightened Jew who had also had a vision, indeed an ultimatum from above, to go and lay hands on the very man who had been violently persecuting his fellow Christ-followers and who had justifiably gotten a reputation as a scourge, someone to avoid at all costs, if you were a secret Christ-follower among the Jews. But that was now many weeks ago, and Saul had gotten word that his fellow travelers had returned to Jerusalem, given a report to the Sanhedrin, and they had immediately sent out several men to investigate what had happened to Saul, the leader of the persecutors of Jesus' disciples. Saul, having learned of this through Ananias, wanted nothing to do with that sort of inquiry, and he knew if he had gone back to Jerusalem with these men, he would have been *persona non grata* not only with the Christ-followers, but also with his fellows on the Sanhedrin and amongst the more hardline Pharisees, who took Phineas as their model of proper zeal for their faith.

No, Saul was now a man without a community, at least in Jerusalem, but he dared not be disobedient to the heavenly vision that had blinded him on Damascus Road. He would never forget that haunting voice that penetrated his very being:

"Saul, Saul why are you persecuting me?" Not "why are you persecuting my people" but "why are you persecuting me?" Such an odd question from one who was himself in heaven, and heavenly in character. Saul had learned through the vision that it was Jesus of Nazareth addressing him—a total shock. If Jesus of Nazareth was in heaven, indeed was God's Son sitting at God's right hand, then Saul was not implementing but rather opposing

---

2. See, e.g., Acts 13:10–11.

DESERT STORM

God's plan of salvation for Jew and Gentile alike. It is a terrible thing for a learned person to learn how very wrong, indeed completely wrong, he had been about something as important as who is the Jewish messiah. And then there was all the guilt that welled up inside Saul when he realized he had been tormenting faithful Jews who had seen better than he had who the messiah really was. The shame of this was profound.

Saul muttered to himself "I should have listened to Gamaliel," but Abram hardly noticed as he trudged on towards the *caravanserai*. While one might think that encountering a heavenly being would simply be a blessing, it had left Saul with eye trouble that would plague him the rest of his life. Rather like Jacob, who was left with a limp after wrestling with one of God's messengers, Saul had a constant reminder in his flesh, a stake in his flesh that God would not take away, of his spiritual blindness in the past about Jesus. It forced a brilliant man to constantly rely on God's grace and not primarily on his own insight and abilities the rest of his life.

"We are not far now from our first stop thanks be to God," said Abram. Abram was a friend of Ananias, and a Christ-follower. He was also something of a traveling salesman who regularly made trips south on the road from Damascus in order to bargain for goods and supplies he would then return to Damascus to sell for a profit. He had a good eye for a good deal, and so in fact he would not mind this journey under normal circumstances. But it was winter, and winter in the desert of Damascus could be cold and cruel, not to mention wet. So far, it had only been windy, but that would change in the days to come. He longed to be home in his house on Straight Street in Damascus cooking some food over an open fire. At the *caravanserai* the food would be poor in quality and expensive too, but Saul had money and was covering all the expenses of this journey.

"Look," said Abram, "I can just make out some torches ahead." The sun had already begun to set, and those torches were not moving so probably they were fixed to the walls of the traveler's rest stop they were approaching. It had already been more than twenty miles of slow traveling this day, but Saul did not seem to mind. His legs were sturdy and firm and there was not a bit of excess flesh anywhere on his body. He also had the virtue of being still a rather young man.[3]

---

3. According to Acts 7:58, Saul was a *neanias* when Stephen was stoned in Jerusalem. This likely means no older than in his early thirties, but it could mean younger than that. A *neanias* is not a child, but it often refers to an unmarried young man. We may guess that Saul was in his early thirties at most when he had his Damascus Road experience somewhere around AD 32–35 depending on when one dates Christ's crucifixion (I favor

The first impression one got of the *caravanserai* when it came into view was of the massive entrance gate leading to an equally large courtyard, where travelers hobbled their horses and beasts of burden for the night. The second impression was of the overwhelming smell of animal dung, particularly camel dung, lying on the ground in steaming piles all around the perimeter of the courtyard. Thankfully, the human accommodations were not in the courtyard, but inside the fortress-like building.

Abram noticed that none of the sights and sounds of the *caravanserai* seemed to surprise or shock Saul, indeed nothing much seemed to draw him out of his introspection. Saul had been deep in thought throughout

---

an April AD 30 date for that event, but it could be as late as April AD 33).

the first day of their journey, and Abram had been loath to interrupt him. Having heard the man speak once in Damascus to the Christ-followers that met in Ananias' house and then in the synagogue there, he could tell immediately that Saul was a highly educated and passionate man, and quite articulate too in talking about his zeal for the God of their fathers.[4] Abram was simply an uneducated tradesman, worldly wise and experienced but barely able to read Aramaic or Greek, and not able to write anything except for signing his name to contracts and receipts. Not so Saul, who carried with him several papyrus rolls in a leather tube, portions of the sacred Scriptures, particularly the prophet Isaiah. Having gotten settled in an alcove within the *caravanserai* and having purchased some warm bowls of soup and some flat bread, Abram and Saul sat down around a brazier with burning embers in it, with shadows playing off against the wall of the alcove. Abram interrupted Saul's reverie and spoke.

"May I ask, why Petra? Why such a long journey down into the land of the Nabateans? I mean there are some other towns along the way, not that I'm complaining, since I do like traveling to Petra and dealing with the merchants there."

After a pause so he could finish slurping his soup, Saul replied, "It's a fair question. It was Ananias who confirmed to me that he, like myself, had had a vision and the voice had told him 'Go! This man [meaning me] is my chosen instrument to proclaim my name to the non-Jews and their kings.' The voice of Jesus had told me that I was simply to go to the nations, but this was an even more specific commission to witness to the non-Jewish kings."

"As you know," Paul continued, "Judaism is not what one would call a missionary religion or an evangelistic religion by and large, though we are very happy to share our faith with the nations if individuals wish to come our way and follow our beliefs and practices and become God-fearers or proselytes. But the commission of Jesus to me, both in my vision and in that of Ananias was to go out and share the paradoxical good news about the crucified and risen Jesus, who is not merely the Jewish messiah but even the Savior and Lord of the world."

Abram was getting impatient with this lengthy explanation, and interrupting said, "Yes, but why Nabatean Arabia, and Petra in particular? Why go there?"

---

4. On his preaching in Damascus, see Acts 9:19–21.

"I'm coming to that, my friend. You see I could not stay in Damascus with the Jewish authorities coming to extradite me to Jerusalem, nor could I simply return to Jerusalem where I would be unwelcome both in the Christ-follower community and to the Jewish authorities as well. Besides which, Damascus is already in Nabatean hands. Witness King Aretas' governor or ethnarch who looks after things in that city for his king. Long story short, I wanted to go somewhere to deal with non-Jews, but those who were well familiar with Jews and the Jewish religion precisely because there had long been trading relationships between Jews and their nearby Semitic neighbors such as the Nabateans and the Idumeans.[5] They were not Greeks, nor were they Romans, but fellow Semites. They were, in a sense, the nearest nations who had not yet heard about Jesus.

"Furthermore, I knew I could practice my trade of leather-working in Petra to support myself and yes, there was a non-Jewish king dwelling there that perhaps I might someday share the good news with."

"So. . . . Let me get this straight. You expect to be able to witness even to King Aretas? You realize that the latest news is that Herod Antipas of Galilee, having divorced Phasaelis and married his brother's wife, is now at war with King Aretas, and Aretas has confiscated some of his land in Perea near the Jordan including the Macherus where John the Baptizer was executed? And furthermore, the Romans are considering reprisals against Aretas.[6] Not perhaps the best of times to try and introduce King Aretas to a new Jewish religion!"

Herod's Macherus fortress was east of the Jordan river.

"You may be right," sighed Paul, "but I cannot be disobedient to the heavenly vision and the commission. I will begin just by sharing with the ordinary folk in Petra, and see where that leads."

"Yes, start small is my advice," said Abram as he shook his head at the boldness and also the determination of Saul. "Anyway, we have at least nine more days of travel if conditions do not get any worse before we get to Petra. Perhaps God will reveal a clearer plan to you when we get nearer to the destination."

"Perhaps," said Saul, "and anyway I am searching the poetic prophecies of Isaiah, which many see as the key to the future of God's people. Have

---

5. The intermingling of these basically Semitic sub-cultures was considerable. Herod the Great himself was partially of Idumean (=Edomite) descent, and King Aretas IV's daughter had been the first wife of Herod Antipas, the son of Herod the Great.

6. In AD 36, there was a plan for Rome to intervene on behalf of Antipas, but it fell by the wayside when Tiberius suddenly died in AD 37.

you noticed how God reveals enough of the future in those prophecies to give us hope, but not so much that we do not have to live by faith each and every day?"

Abram groaned and said, "Those prophecies are complex and beyond my understanding. But yes we journey in faith, especially in a sandstorm when you can hardly see your hand in front of your face!"

Saul wrinkled his nose and finally cracked a smile, "So right my new friend, so right. Let's get some rest as I suspect tomorrow will be a long day as well."

"OK, but first I had better talk to you a bit about the Nabateans. I'll grab us a couple of cups of wine, and I will tell the tale."

Saul smiled and nodded his consent, for he truly did not know much about the Nabateans and their story.

The Nabatean Kingdom

Our story is set in what may be an unfamiliar location for many readers.[7] Paul of *Arabia*. Just where in the world is Arabia? Such a term can be confusing if not properly located and defined. Most of us have geographical amnesia and especially so when it comes to unfamiliar places and even more so for ancient lands. Arabia was the term that the Romans used to refer to the land that lay just south and east of Roman Palestine. An area of land nestled in between Egypt and Syria. For those familiar with the Old Testament, it included the regions of Edom and Moab and the Negev. In modern terms it would have included southern Syria, Jordan, and the northwest corner of Saudia Arabia.[8] From seaports to semi-arid deserts, this was a diverse territory both in terms of geographical zones and cultural aspects. The spoken language appears to be Nabatean, a dialect of Aramaic. Thousands of graffiti attest to the prevalence of this as the majority language. Although this region was called Arabia, it does not appear that any ancient form of Arabic was spoken during this period.[9] Likewise, although its origins are in the Hellenistic period, nearly all of the inscriptions and coins are in Nabatean. Greek and bilingual inscriptions are very rare.[10]

---

7. Indeed, until relatively recently Roman Arabia was an area of neglect in Roman studies but has in recent decades become an area of intense scrutiny. See Isaac, "Inscriptions," 334–41.

8. Bowersock, *Roman Arabia*, 1.

9. Millar, *Roman Near East*, 402–3. See his discussion on the difficulty of the question and the lack of probability.

10. Millar, *Roman Near East*, 402–3. Cf. Isaac, "Inscriptions," *in Near East Under*

Who were the Nabateans? Most date the kingdom from 168 BC with their first king, Aretas I to Rabell II in AD 106, when the Roman Emperor Trajan annexes them as a formal Roman province. The Nabateans were a powerful dynasty that lasted over two centuries with origins in the late Hellenistic period. They first enter the pages of history in the aftermath of Alexander's death when his former general Antigonus wanted to add to his growing empire. In 312 BC, he decided to send troops to take over the Nabateans, unsuccessfully. One of the great strengths of the region in that vast and arid landscape was the ability to see for long distances. News of troops on the way quickly spread, and the Nabateans prepared. They convinced the Greeks that there was no good reason to overtake their kingdom since they had no resources that they desired.[11] At their height, during the late first century BC, the main cities would include Petra, Bostra, and Damascus. During the Roman period, they seem to have had some degree of autonomy. They first encountered Rome in 64 BC in the campaigns of Pompey, who annexed Syria and made Nabatea a client-kingdom, just like Judea. Such annexation helped the Romans who probably thought of Nabatea as a buffer zone between them and their feared enemies, the Parthians.[12] The history of the Nabatean territory and Rome is diverse. At one point, Antony gives Judea and Arabia to Cleopatra as a gift.[13] Herod is forced by Cleopatra, via Antony, to invade and attack the Nabatean kingdom. However, with Judea annexed by 14 AD, the Nabateans enter into their "golden age" under King Aretas IV. The most famous king, his coins bear the title "lover of his people" probably reflecting the prosperous growth under his reign.[14]

The origins of the Nabateans are hard to decipher, but they first appear as nomads who settled in this region and grew immensely wealthy from their trade along the spice route. The Nabateans had risen to international prominence for their fame and wealth from their vast trading networks. They were known as one of the "great trading peoples of the Near East."[15] They appear to have traded many products ranging from oils, balms, incense such as frankincense and myrrh, ivory, sugar, gems and stones, and even exotic wildlife. They also were merchants who helped supply the desires of wealthy and elite Greek and Romans.[16] This kingdom was connected by trading outposts that

---

Roman Rule, 334–41.

11. Bowersock, *Roman Arabia*, 14.
12. Bryce, *Ancient Syria*, 242.
13. Bowersock, *Roman Arabia*, 41. Cf. Plutarch, *Ant.*, 36.2.
14. Bowersock, *Roman Arabia*, 59.
15. Bryce, *Ancient Syria*, 241.
16. Bryce, *Ancient Syria*, 241.

included a port on the Red Sea and various outposts in the desert, connecting it to the Sinai peninsula in the south. In the north, from Damascus, they had access to the Mediterranean. So great was their fame that they were known by the Hahn Dynasty in China.

The kingdom was a combination of both villages and cities of varying populations. With its origins in a nomadic lifestyle, villages remained popular. However, large cities such as Petra (ancient *Raqmu*) and Bostra were formidable powerhouses in their own right. The establishment and construction of Petra appear to have begun around the turn of the first century. Petra is famous for the Khazneh and its dazzling rock-cut facade, complete with Corinthian columns that loom over both ancient and modern visitors. The site also houses a main theater and a statue of Aretas IV who most likely began the construction of the Khazneh in the early first century.[17] Commonly known as "the treasury," it was the traditional entry to the city and was sure to have made an impact just as it does today. Although called a treasury, it was more likely a temple or a tomb of some sort. The actual purpose remains a mystery. There were also legal precincts.[18] The city is located in the *Wadi Musa* or Valley of Moses, where Arab tradition holds that Moses hit the rock and water gushed forth.[19] The near-perfect natural barriers and access to freshwater through two springs—an essential point of survival for anyone in the ancient world—led to its prominence and longevity.

---

17. Millar, *Roman Near East*, 406.
18. Bowersock, *Roman Arabia*, 61.
19. Bryce, *Ancient Syria*, 243.

CHAPTER TWO

THE NOMADIC NABATEANS

Throwing a few more limbs in the brazier, Abram handed over an ample-sized wine goblet to Saul, having just poured out wine from a wineskin he carried with him whenever he traveled.

"We have a grape arbor back in Damascus, and it produces wonderful red wine, which we get the benefit of now."

"L'chaim" (to life), said Abram, as they quaffed some of the best wine Saul had ever tasted.

"This is far better than those Jerusalem wines, and perhaps even the equal of the famed Falernian wine my family used to drink in Tarsus," replied Saul, as he licked his lips.

"So, about the Nabateans, they have a long history, but they have managed not to have their story told in our sacred texts, not even in the history chronicles involving Samuel and David."

"Why is that, do you suppose?" asked Saul.

"Well, these people were nomads, Bedouins of a sort, and they came from far south in the Arabian peninsula. At first they were simply nomads, but eventually they founded some impressive cities like Petra their capital.[1] Some have even suggested they came from Sheba of Solomon fame, but probably not. Their language is clearly some kind of Semitic language like Hebrew, but they have their own script which they write from right to left, and unlike Hebrew there are no jots and tittles."

"How odd," said Paul, "It must be a difficult language to decipher."

---

1. See Josephus, *J.W.* 5.4.3; *Ant.* 18.5.1.

"I can't say anything about deciphering their script, but aurally there are enough words that sound like Aramaic or Hebrew and have similar meanings, for example '*salim*' is their word for 'peace' just as *shalom* is ours. In any case, being Bedouins they were originally tenders of flocks, which is why they moved around in the desert looking for oases and grass for the flocks. So far as I can discover, they began to be a distinguishable people about the time of the rise of the Persian empire, and then Cyrus' reign. In other words, Judeans were still in exile when these people began to make a name for themselves on the stage of known history. Their gods (and yes they believe in multiple deities like most everyone except us) seem to be the gods from southern Arabia, although there are some similarities in their paired male and female deities with gods you find in Egypt, like Isis and Serapis."

"Perhaps they were trading partners with Egypt in the centuries before the Hasmoneans?"

"Perhaps so. I can't say for sure. What I can say is that they also have some very distinctive deities such as Atargatis, whose temple you will no doubt see in Petra. The Nabateans are a very religious people, and they don't take kindly to people criticizing their beliefs. Fair warning in advance."

"Duly noted," said Saul, but Abram could tell this was not going to deter his companion from his mission. "I'll have to use my best persuasive skills and rely on the Holy Spirit to convict them."

Abram continued, "That you will. The Nabateans are now traders with all sorts of peoples, peoples from the far east who come to the ports the Nabateans have on the Red Sea, peoples who come overland on roads from Persia following the Silk Road, and of course the Egyptians and the Syrians and others. They have a large prosperous commercial enterprise which has allowed them to build some major cities and fortresses. Even south of Gaza they built a city in the desert, but more on that later. Here let me draw you something of a rough map of the area, and the trade routes in the sand here."

PAUL OF ARABIA

THE NOMADIC NABATEANS

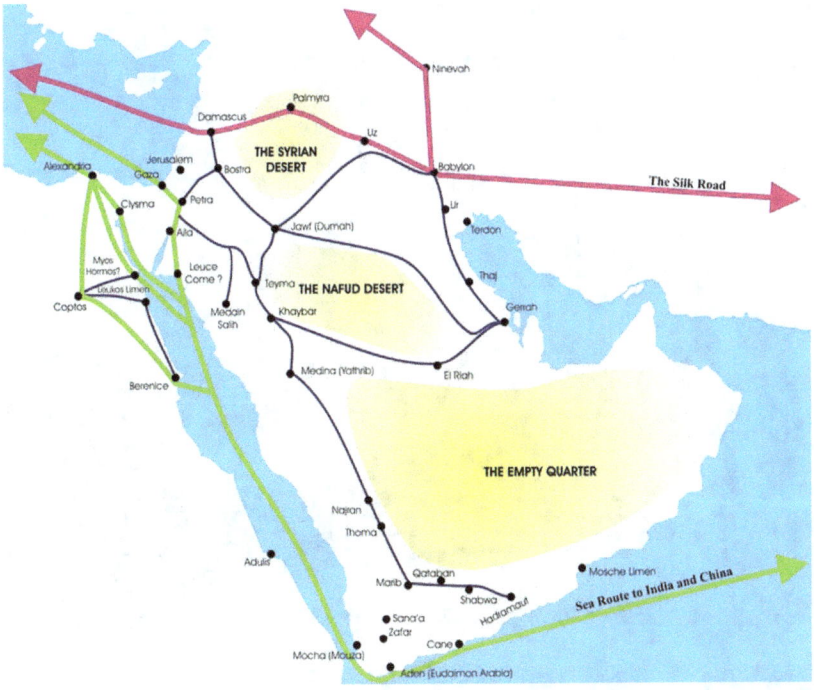

Abram continued: "Today the capital city of Petra is thriving, with some 20,000 residents and lots of regular traffic and business passing through it. But I'd better get on with talking to you about King Aretas, which is his throne name (from the Greek word 'arete' which of course means excellence—hence 'His Excellency'). He is the fourth ruler in a row in Nabatea to take this title. The Nabateans became major players in the region as early as King Obodas I who had major victories over both the Hasmoneans, squelching their expansionistic dreams of taking more territory east of the Jordan, but also successfully fighting off the Seleucids as well. They are formidable fighters, and not to be trifled with! It was Obadas who successfully took control of part of the Negev south of Gaza and built the fortress city of Avdat[2]—

---

2. It was the most important city on the Incense Route after Petra, between the first century BC and the seventh century AD. It was founded in the third century BC, and inhabited by Nabateans, Romans, and Byzantines. Avdat was a seasonal camping ground for Nabatean caravans traveling along the early Petra–Gaza road (Darb es-Sultan) in the third to late second century BC. The city's original name was changed to Avdat in honor of Nabatean King Obodas I, who, according to tradition, was revered as a deity and was buried there.

Getting Places: Travel in the Roman World

People are always on the move from one place to another. Such was true to some extent in the ancient world. Although travel to far and remote areas has increased during our time, travel was part of the ancient world as well. Circumstances and economics can dictate travel. Some are forced to travel as a result of war, famine, or slavery. Apart from those circumstances, travel abroad would not be possible for many due to economic reasons. We must understand that many, if not a majority of ancient persons, lived, and died in a small geographic region. Apart from these groups, the groups that did the most traveling in the ancient world were most likely technical workers and armies. Often depicted traveling in classical literature are groups like healers, theater or play workers, or skilled laborers such as glassblowers or metalworkers who move to find work.[3] Likewise, armies would be on the move from place to place in the ancient world as a result of wars and conquest. Some would travel for religious or medical reasons as well. One thinks of various Jewish groups making a pilgrimage to Jerusalem for the various festivals. Medical travel was also popular, where travelers would navigate to a temple of Asclepius or the region of a known medical healer (see Closer Look on Medicine). Depending on the socio-economic level, many would travel for educational opportunities with Rome, Alexandria, and Tarsus as common educational destinations. Those higher up the political order probably traveled more often as well, notably the emperors of Rome traveled extensively.

Travel was either by land or by sea, and both provided their own dangers. During the Roman Empire, and in some part needed for successful expansion, the Roman period was more secure than previous empires. Real and perceived threats still existed. The rise of travel in this period also gave rise to various taverna or inns and related places for the consumption of food (see Closer Look on Dining and Food).

There were four main transportation routes. As Everett Ferguson has shown there were two by land and two by sea. The primary sea route was from Ostia to Puteoli to Alexandria, Egypt, and mainly used by merchants to pick up grain. The second major sea route began on land from the Appian way but ended up going through Corinth by ship and connecting to various locales. There was also a route to Corinth and then on to Ephesus. From there, one gained access to much of Asia Minor by land routes. Finally, one could travel across the Adriatic and via the Egnatian way cross over Macedonia into Asia. As Ferguson notes, the most valued trade route in Early Christianity was the route between Corinth and Ephesus.[4]

Some distances necessitated travel by sea. If one chose to travel by sea, various sizes of ships were available. The largest type of vessel was most likely the grain freighters that went straight across the "Mare Nostrum" to Alexandria and back. Other large boats included the *trireme* that was used to transport troops from region to region using a combination of oarsmen

3. OCD, 1547.
4. Ferguson, *Backgrounds*, 86–87.

and sails. For travel and trade, smaller ships were used and typically consisted of one sail made of linen or leather.[5] Often, travelers could find a ship to carry them by paying a low fare. How did sea travelers know how to get from place to place? Most sea travel relied on following a coastline or moving from one fixed point on land to another. Sometimes, the stars or the moon also provided navigational help. Expertise on local conditions was also needed to know where rocks and shallow reefs might lie. Maps were not widely used for sea travel. Several threats to sea travel existed from weather conditions which made shipwrecks familiar to piracy on the open waters. Sea travel was restricted to specific months as the winter weather saw an increase in storms and travel became more hazardous due to poor visibility. Common knowledge was that no one was supposed to sail from October 15 to March 15. Wide-scale piracy also appears to be a known threat to ancient sea travel. Often pirates operated on the fringes and had strategic attacks. The advent of the Roman period under Augustus saw safer waters as the Roman control over the coastline allowed it to stamp out piracy on a broader scale.[6]

If one chose not to take the risks of sea travel, then travel by land was the only option. Land travel was often by wheeled transport. Carts and wagons were the vehicles of choice for this type of travel to move both persons and cargo across long distances. Various animals such as horses, large oxen, donkeys, or mules were used to pull the vehicle. Single travel passengers would also use camels or horses for travel travel during the Roman period.

Travel was substantially helped by the extensive road system developed by the Roman Empire. The first stretches of the great Appian way were undertaken around 312 BC, and by the time of 147 BC, the road system was connected to Cisalpine Gaul.[7] The vast networks of roads intended initially to move Roman troops also provided a network of connections between various Roman cities. One estimation puts the total number of miles of roads at 53,000 miles.[8] Famous roads included the Via Appia and the Via Egnatia. The Appian way stretched from the south of Rome to Capua ran angularly through Italy to the Adriatic coast. The famous via Egnatia ran from the west coast of Greece to Neapolis and towards Byzantium. It connected the Adriatic Sea to the Aegean Sea.

The early Roman emperors continued the massive road-building project with notable highways constructed under the reigns of Augustus and Claudi

---

5. *OCD*, 1400.
6. *OCD*, 1185.
7. *OCD*, 1320.
8. Ferguson, *Backgrounds*, 88.

> us.⁹ Land travel was much easier due to the widespread use of extensive maps. The spreading of the Roman Empire and desire to know the extent of the empire contributed to map-making, complete with milestones. One danger with travel via road was the constant danger of bandits or robbers that might lay in wait for travelers. Although Rome tried to rid the land of bandits, like they had done with pirates on the sea, but they were never entirely successful. One is immediately reminded of the story of the Good Samaritan (Luke 10:25–37), which seems to reflect relatively common perceptions of the dangers of ancient travel. Paul likewise experiences much of what was typical of ancient travel: relying on the hospitality of a network of friends and family, extensive travels by road (Acts 13–15), by sea (Acts 20–21), and even during a shipwreck (Acts 27–28).

Paul interrupted Abram and said, "I'm beginning to get a feeling you're trying to tell me to be cautious in what I do and say while in Petra."

"You are wise beyond words in drawing that conclusion," said Abram with a grin. "I wouldn't want your mission for Christ to have an unnecessarily premature ending. Like many another great ruler, Aretas IV uses coins as propaganda, showing images of himself and his Queen Shakkat." Reaching in his robe he took a coin out from his money bag which was tied to his belt.

---

9. *OCD*, 1320.

Note the writing on the obverse side of this coin, which looks something like paleo-Hebrew. The image on the front of the coin appears to be Atargatis.

This statue of Atargatis was moved from Petra to the new museum in Amman.

"Is it really true, that Aretas IV has successfully expanded his territory so far north that he now even has *control* over Damascus?" asked Saul.

"Yes, that is correct," says Abram, "though it is more like a controlling interest, with a representative governor there. It is not a city controlled by the Romans."

By now both men had drunk all the wine that had been in the wineskin and were beginning to get sleepy. "That's probably more than enough Nabatean lore for one night," Saul said, "but I'm much obliged for filling in the gaps in my knowledge. I shall endeavor to tread carefully while there. One last thing—are there Jews in Petra?"

"Oh yes, but not enough for a quorum and a synagogue," replied Abram, "And now we must retire, that is if the braying of the camels will quiet down a bit." There was much traveling still to do, if Saul and Abram were to reach the Rose City before the darkest and wettest and coldest days of winter descended on the region.

This stone, found in Madaba in Jordan but now in the Vatican, is in Nabatean script and indicates that Aretas IV ruled during the time of Paul the apostle, from before his conversion until the late 30s.

CHAPTER THREE

ALIENS AND ALLIES, SLAVES AND THIEVES

THE AMOUNT OF TRAFFIC ON THE SPICE ROAD IN INCLEMENT WEATHER surprised Saul. There were whole families on the road, traveling north and south, Roman and Nabatean soldiers as well, businessmen too, camel caravans carrying all sorts of foodstuffs, spices, amphorae of wine, and most any commodity that would sell.

Saul remarked, "I'm used to what happens to traffic on the water, not what happens in a land-locked place like this. Normally, all the small boats stop making any journeys of any significant distance in the eighth Roman month of the year[1] and they do not resume travel until the Ides of the month named after Mars, as spring begins to happen and the prevailing winds change. Obviously, no one pays attention to such factors when traveling in winter on a major road like this."

"You are right. Most surprising is whole families, even small children traveling under these conditions, but some of them have no choice, being displaced by war or famine or the like." Just then they passed a slave trader with ten dark-skinned slaves chained together heading north, to be sold presumably in Damascus.

"They are Ethiopians probably, and they've already had a long journey to get to this point, captured somewhere south of Egypt, shipped across the Red Sea to a Nabatean port, and then led north through Petra and points north, if, that is, they weren't simply bought in the slave market in Petra.

1. I.e., mid-October.

Either way, their original point of origin is Ethiopia, and they are highly prized for their strength and endurance in the mines, rowing grain freighters, and much more."

"Slavery," said Saul and he spat. "It should be distasteful to every Jew in view of our own history in Egypt. Our own sacred texts tell us how demeaning and demanding life becomes when humans created in God's image are treated as mere property or chattel."

"Yes, well," said Abram, "but it is the way of the world, and you might be surprised how many Jews who do not live in Jerusalem or Judea actually have slaves. Movable property, it is called, and did you notice they are all branded, like the mark of Cain, so everyone will know they are or were slaves."

The donkey Abram was pulling along was protesting vigorously at the pace they were keeping, not least because it was carrying not only supplies but also the tools of Saul's trade of leather working, a cooking pot, a small tent which two persons could hunker down in if necessary, some wineskins, a container of clothes, some charcoal to start a fire with, and much more. No one could take an arduous ten-day journey without supplies and stopping along the way, especially not in winter.

Saul was wearing both a tunic as an undergarment and a large black cloak on top of that with a hood, and Abram was dressed similarly. No one would recognize or be able to pick them out as persons who were notable or notorious. They appeared to be the average travelers. The thin sun was trying to break through the prevailing clouds with little success, and there was enough dust in the air that one constantly felt like one was in a dream-like state, with persons and animals suddenly appearing out of the haze to their right. All of a sudden, the donkey, whom Abram ironically called Balaam, stopped dead in his tracks.

Looming before them were two men riding on camels wearing interesting turbans of a sort.

"Persian astrologers probably," suggested Abram, "the so-called Magi, who are counselors to kings. But why would they be heading North? The nearest king is Aretas in Petra."

"Perhaps he is sending them on a negotiation mission. I hear Herod Antipas is suing for peace after having divorced his first wife, Aretas' daughter, and then losing some of his territory in and around Pella to Aretas' formidable army. These honor challenge situations can lead to all sorts of catastrophes, and Herod is hoping for damage control I suppose."

"You could be right," nodded Abram, "I hadn't thought about that."

The second day's journey involved traveling almost thirty Roman miles, so when Saul and Abram arrived at their traveler's rest stop they were well and truly worn out, ready for a meal and bed.

At this rest stop, both men noticed a whole lot more chatter about the Nabatean army sending more troops North. Something was up, and it wasn't just peace negotiations with Herod in Galilee. Were the Nabateans expanding their territory to the North? It was certainly possible. They had been known to be a largely peaceful people and good trade partners unless messed with by outsiders. Some four centuries before the time of Jesus of Nazareth, Antigonus, one of Alexander the Great's noblemen, attacked the Nabateans during a religious celebration outside Petra. Antigonus and his army tried to steal the goods stored in Petra and kidnapped a lot of the people. However, this ended up being an unsuccessful endeavor and served only to prove the underlying strength of the peaceful Nabateans. Aretas IV however seemed to have some expansionistic ambitions.[2]

The next eight days of the journey were characterized by monotony as both these two men and their beast got used to trudging along to Petra. There was some safety in numbers in traveling with others, and oddly enough, it was at the so-called safe havens, the caravanserais and rest stops at oases that they had to watch their possessions carefully due to thieves being present.

One night Saul awoke with a start to discover someone quietly trying to pilfer some things out of the saddle bag on Balaam the donkey. Saul jumped from the ground and ran towards the donkey and immediately the thief fled into the night. Abram, meanwhile was snoring away and never woke up. "He's a good guide" muttered Saul to himself, "but not much of a guard. Time to go back to sleep."

Slavery and the Roman World

One of the tragic aspects of the history of humanity is the widespread dehumanization of people across space and time. The owning of other human

---

2. It is in connection with this attack by Antigonus that the Nabateans are first mentioned in the historical records in the year 312 BC. It would not be until the early second century AD, about 107, that the Nabatean kingdom would be incorporated in the Roman Empire as a province called Arabia Petraea. The Nabateans were not even client kings of Rome in Paul's day, but also they were not feared by the Romans in the same way the Parthians in the East were.

beings is a scourge on the history of the human race and reveals one of the devastating realities of human evil. Oppression and cruelty are a common feature of every major empire, and people-group and the world of Paul was sadly no different. Paul lived in an enslaved society. Put more specifically, many people that Paul met and knew personally were slaves. The early Christian movement was made up of a cross-section of the ancient world, and the world of Paul included many slaves.[3] Estimates are notoriously hard to come by. The influential historian Walter Scheidel put the number at 10 percent of the empire's population or 6 million slaves out of 60 million in the empire during the late first century. Although he acknowledged this was a low estimate. More recent work has increased that percentage to 20–30 percent of the population, depending on the location.[4] More than sheer numbers, grotesque as those are, more debilitating is the perception of the broader ancient world as a slave society where there were no groups untouched by slavery. One difficulty is that most of the existing evidence—other than material culture—is written by the slaveholders, and little remains from the viewpoint of slaves.

The ancient world simply assumed that slavery was a part of the order of human society. Going back as far as Aristotle, slaves are "human tools."[5] Romans and Greeks disagreed on the definition of slavery. For Greeks, like Aristotle, there was a theory of "natural slaves." Not so for Romans, for them, slavery was "against nature," and slavery was a part of the law of nations, and, contrary to nature, someone was brought under the power of someone else.[6] Ancient Roman law differentiated between not only slave and free, but even freed persons who were born free (*ingenui*) and those who gained their freedom by manumission from slavery (*libertini*).

Was Slavery Focused on One Group?

Unlike slavery in the ante-bellum period of America, slavery was not solely born by one group. Nearly every non-Roman group could be enslaved. If one could be conquered, one could be enslaved. Most became slaves through Roman conquest, although some kidnapping occurred, and others were born into slavery. For example, on one occasion, Julius Caesar enslaved nearly one million inhabitants of Gaul and sent them back to Italy.[7] If one extrapolates from

---

3. Judge, *Social Distinctives of the Christians*, 1–56; Meeks, *First Urban Christians*, 51–73.

4. Joshel, *Slavery in the Roman World*, 8. See also Garnsey and Saller, *Roman Empire*, 83–85.

5. Aristotle, *Pol.* 1.1253b.

6. Harrill, "Paul and Slavery," 576.

7. Plutarch, *Caes.* 15.3, cited in Harrill, "Paul and Slavery," 579.

the massive expansion of empire through the first centuries by Julius Caesar and Augustus, one can begin to imagine the enormous number of slaves pouring into the port cities of Ostia and even Corinth to the slave markets for sale. Slaves would be set up in the market on a platform that rotated so that they could be inspected. They often stood with a sign that indicated their place of origin, any defects, and possibly any unique skills.

The slave population in ancient Rome not only increased through war but also through the reproduction of slaves, where the children born to a slave mother became slaves as well. Infants left to exposure were also a source for slaves. Given the patriarchal reality of the ancient world, female children were less valued than male children.[8] Further, children with physical defects were also neglected. Infant exposure was when unwanted babies would be left either on trash dumps or in temples to be picked up by slave traders. Male children became physical laborers, and female children were often forced into prostitution. Early Christians would eventually rescue such unwanted children, raising them as their own.

Particularly devastating was the fact that slave status erased all sense of personal identity. The slave had no nation, no ancestors, no past. They were outsiders to society.[9] As outsiders, they were vulnerable to mistreatment and injustice. They could not only be beaten, but all injuries were not injuries to them, but their owners. Sexual exploitation was also common, both of male and female slaves. Slaves were given nicknames, like moderns name their pets, for example Onesimus means "useful," and Eutychus means "lucky."

Could Slaves Find Freedom?

In contrast to more modern forms of slavery, Roman slavery did allow for the possibility of freedom. However, it is important to remember that manumission is different than emancipation. Still, once a freed-person, more rights and privileges were granted to the ex-slave. For example, they often became Roman citizens, had their marriage recognized, could buy and sell property, and could sue others. Sandra Joshel has argued, if slavery was social death, then "manumission was a sort of social 'rebirth'" (although not a complete one).[10] Manumission took various forms in the Roman Empire: from public and private manumissions to full and limited manumissions.

Humiliation followed those who gained manumission, as the stigma of slavery did not leave them behind. Freed persons still had to show *obsequiem*

---

8. Harris, "Child-Exposure in the Roman Empire"; Tate, "Christianity and the Legal Status of Abandoned Children," 123–41.

9. Joshel, *Slavery in the Roman World*, 38.

10. Joshel, *Slavery in the Roman World*, 42.

(deference or obedience) to their former owner, who now became their patron. They also could still owe their owner some level of work.[11] No longer a slave, the person was now a client of a patron. During the reign of Nero, the senate debated if they should re-enslave those freedmen who had not shown proper *obsequiem* to their former masters. Nero ultimately dismissed the case.[12] But such shows the peril and ever reaching tentacles of slavery in the ancient world, even post manumission.

Where Would One Find Slaves?

Slaves were found at all levels of production in the ancient world ranging from the mines, to the farmlands, to businesses and homes. From the lowest rungs of society to the highest echelons in Caesar's household, slaves were found at every level. Because of the sheer number of available slaves, they were found at most economic levels as well. Slaves were found across the social spectrum. The lowest and most brutal conditions were the mines where they were worked to death. More common was the domestic and farm slaves found throughout the Roman Empire. At the top of the social ladder would have been the slaves of emperor who had immense power, privilege, and status. Sometimes, even more so than freed persons. It was not only the elite who owned slaves. Although someone of the elite political class could have hundreds of slaves, those of lesser means might have one or two.

In contrast again to modern slavery, Roman educated slaves were highly prized. Some persons enslaved by the Romans were already literate, some even well educated. In addition, slaves in the Roman world could receive training and education, taking up positions such as artisans, teachers, philosophers, and physicians. Because of the training, slaves could also earn a small wage, known as a *peculium*. Sometimes these assets, although technically still belonging to their master, could be used to secure their manumission.[13] While slavery in antiquity differed from modern forms of slavery in Europe and America, in all cases it was an attempt to own other human beings and make them do various tasks for the owner, often tasks the Roman elites did not want to get their hands dirty with. In this context, a Pauline letter like Philemon shows that Paul knew the problems with this institution and was working for the manumission of slaves like Onesimus not least because 'he should be received no longer as a slave, but as more than a slave, a brother in Christ.'

---

11. Harrill, "Paul and Slavery," 580.
12. Hermann-Otto, "Slaves and Freedmen," 69.
13. Harrill, "Paul and Slavery," 583.

CHAPTER FOUR

ARRIVAL AT THE ROSE CITY

"... BUT I WENT INTO ARABIA. LATER I RETURNED TO DAMASCUS. THEN after three years, I went up to Jerusalem."—Gal 1:17–18

Like many ancient cities (see e.g., Hierapolis) you got to the city of the living by means of walking through the city of the dead—the necropolis. A large necropolis meant many generations of peoples had lived and died in a particular city. Such was the case with Petra, whose very name conjures up a city carved out of pure rock. Actually, Petra is the Greek name for the city, but the native Nabateans called it *Raqmu*, though it may be the same city referred to as *Seir* or even *Sela* in ancient Egyptian records.

Because the Nabateans were a desert people, they were quite able in defending themselves as well as fending for themselves when necessary. They were skilled in collecting rain and spring water, carving things, including residences and tombs, out of the sandstone in the desert, and living off their flocks of sheep and goats and some minimal agriculture.

Entering the city from the north as Saul and Abram did, one had to pass through a narrow corridor or dry ravine downhill for about three quarters of a Roman mile before the scene opened up into a large market area. Along the way, Saul and Abram saw many tombs carved into the cliffs, a water channel bringing water to the center of the city, and a shrine to Atargatis, where pilgrims were expected to stop and pay homage to the Nabatean goddess.

The entrance to what today is called the Siq. Notice the fig tree growing out of the rock wall, due to the water channel there.

ARRIVAL AT THE ROSE CITY

The water conduits

The shrine of Atargatis near the entranceway to Petra.

When Abram and Saul came to the opening in the ravine where they could see people and shops and camels sitting down, Saul wanted to go immediately to a booth where he saw leather goods and tents for sale.

Abram cautioned patience. "There will be plenty enough time later today for that. Let me first give you the tour and show you what is here."

The first glimpse of the city beyond the Siq

ARRIVAL AT THE ROSE CITY

While this is what this area looks like today, scholars have become convinced that the so-called treasury building seen here, is in fact the tomb of Aretas IV, and Paul would not have seen this when he came to Petra.

The sheer size of the necropolis was simply jaw-dropping. Saul had never seen so many tombs carved out of sheer rock, indeed out of a rock cliff in the middle of Petra. Then there was the gigantic temple started by Obadas long ago. . . .

"It's important for me to tell you that the Nabateans are dedicated polytheists, and what I mean by that is that they do not take kindly to people telling them their gods are not real gods, or that there is only one God, and it's not one of theirs. If you plan on sharing the gospel here, I suggest no open air proclamations, but rather just one-on-one witnessing, perhaps when you come into contact with people buying tents or leather goods from you. Safest would be to only evangelize people who are purchasing things here in Petra, but are just passing through up or down the spice road. Remember, there is no synagogue here, and Aretas is already upset with that Jewish ruler in Galilee, Herod Antipas. Try and make some friends while you are here."

Saul listened intently, while stroking his beard. "In other words, you're telling me open evangelism will likely lead to a short stay here, or even being brought before the authorities. But I'm a Roman citizen, doesn't that give me some status and immunity?"

"Not here, brother," replied Abram, "you are not in the Roman Empire here. You might as well be in exile in Babylon."

Saul sighed and said, "Well, I'm hoping to stay for a good while so I'll ponder your advice."

"You better do more than ponder. You better take my advice as your friend and fellow Christ-follower." At that juncture, Abram said, "Let's climb up that big slope over there and see al Deir, where the story goes Obadas himself used to banquet and hold symposiums."

The climb involved some 500 steps straight up, and even a seasoned traveler like Saul found himself somewhat winded when he reached the top, and as they were turning the last corner Saul said to Abram, "This better be worth all this effort," and no sooner were the words out of his mouth than he saw the amazing building carved out of a sandstone cliff, and his jaw hung open for a good while.

"That's quite a dining room!" exclaimed the apostle to the gentiles.

"Yes, Nabateans never much liked doing things half way or small." It was clear to Saul that he had much to learn about the Nabateans, and as is so often the case when one has not studied something, or had regular contact with a people, it is easy to underestimate their accomplishments or how formidable a people they might be. Saul was learning he needed a short course in all things Nabatean.

"Well, at least," said Saul, "they speak the international language of trade and travel, Greek."

"Yes, but if that's all you use in conversation here, they will soon know you are an alien, a foreigner." Saul and Abram spent the rest of the afternoon looking for accommodations that Saul could rent. They found a place carved out of the side of the mountain next to the giant temple built by Obadas. Saul paid in advance several month's rent.

"Seriously, how long do you plan to stay here?"

"I suppose the answer to that depends on how successful I am in recruiting people to follow Christ. But I've prepared myself mentally to be here for a considerable period of time. It will take a considerable period before I'm ready to return to Jerusalem, although fortunately my sister and her nephew live there."[1]

---

1. Acts 23:16.

"I suggest you come back to Damascus first before going up to Jerusalem. Either Ananias or I will be able to tell you what the lay of the land is in Jerusalem before you make that journey. And you might want to change your appearance when you do go up to Zion."

"OK," said Saul, "that's a wise idea. Though I could follow the trade route from here to Gaza and then up to Jerusalem, showing up there unannounced might not be a very intelligent move."[2]

"And now my friend we should have some food, and then I must pack, as I'll be leaving with my purchases by late morning. You no doubt saw the leather working shop in the market area, so I'm assuming you will approach them tomorrow and make a start here."

"Yes, that's my plan, and I am deeply grateful to you for all your help and guidance since we left Damascus. I shall try to make some friends here and to stay a good while. Who knows, perhaps I will even have occasion to speak with King Aretas?"

"That's probably over-optimistic, since he's busy with his military activities, but only God knows what comes next."

"Too true my friend, too true." Their dinner was a quiet one, and Saul being gregarious and outgoing knew he would miss Abram. The dinner of lamb shish kabob and bread and wine was followed by a good night's rest in Saul's new home.

---

2. On the trade routes from Petra, see pp. 11–17 above.

CHAPTER FIVE

SOLITARY SAUL

Petra was less than half the size of Jerusalem, but as a major crossroads for trade, there were plenty of business opportunities in this place. Although the main trade was in spices and the like, a desert people had great respect for those who could make high quality tents, the portable dwellings needed by nomads. And Saul was precisely such a person.

The weak winter sun was shining in the market place when Saul approached an elderly man who ran a leather-working shop and business. He had learned from Abram, whom he had said his farewells too only an hour before, that the man's name was Alexander, a Greek name. This augured well, thought Saul.

"Kurie,"[1] said Saul, bowing slightly, "might I have a word with you?"

"Certainly," said Alexander, "I see you speak Greek."

"Indeed, I grew up in Tarsus in a Greek-speaking family. I've come here to make a fresh start. My family were leather-workers, including making the famous *cilicium*, goat's hair cloth tents. This is in fact how we were granted Roman citizenship, making tents for the legions stationed there. I am looking for work, and I hear your shop makes the finest leather goods and tents anywhere around here. I wondered if you could use a seasoned leather worker like myself?"

"It must be the gods who sent you my way, for I have been desperate for more help, so much has trade increased here at this desert crossroads town. We have people coming from the ports, people coming from the

---

1. While this word can be translated "lord" in a context like this it normally is just a term of respect, rather like the English word "sir."

desert, people coming from Damascus and other points north, it is a busy place. While we don't have a full complement of Greek-styled games, we do have a major theater here, which includes both drama and sport performances of various sorts, and people come from near and far to see it. The need to rent tents is considerable, though not so much at this time of year. But come spring that's another story."

The theater at Petra. Notice that it is a Greek style theater with a *skene* or stage area for dramatic performances.

"Excellent," said Saul, "I would be honored to be in your employ, and of course would expect to demonstrate my skills before you contemplated what you would pay me. I do have two small samples of my work with me, there is first of all my leather satchel I have on my shoulder here." Saul used it to carry his precious possessions such as his papyri and writing implements. "And here's a wineskin. I came from Damascus, and did not bring a tent with me, but my greatest skill is in making tents. I am also literate, and good at bookkeeping, keeping records of credits and debits."[2]

---

2. Too seldom stressed is that Paul's letters are replete with business language not court room language. For example, in Rom 4:13–25 Paul speaks of Abraham's trust in God being *reckoned* as righteousness. This is the language of the reckoning of credits and debits, of business, not the language of judges and law courts. Paul was not a lawyer, he

Alexander's pale blue eyes had been staring intently at Saul while he made his little speech and demonstration, trying to discern, rather like Diogenes, whether Saul was an honest man and could be trusted.

"Just so you know, I am a Jew most recently from Damascus, hard-working, and a man for whom his word is his bond. If you want to hire me first on a trial basis, I'm fine with that. I'm just looking for good honest work to pay for my cost of living here. I've rented rooms down near the temple."

Alexander stroked his chin, and said "Very well. You may come first thing in the morning, and we will see how things go. I've worked with Jews before in other cities, and they were hard-working and honest, though I didn't much understand their religion."

"Excellent," said Saul grinning, "I will be here first thing in the morning. Perhaps you can tell me where the best place is to buy foodstuffs. I do my own cooking."

"Certainly, right across the square from this shop is an excellent fruit and nut and bread shop, and right next to it, the wine shop."

Saul spent the rest of the day familiarizing himself with the lay of the town, the coins used in trade, the places to buy this or that kind of food or wine. He did a little shopping for non-perishable goods, and he began to settle into the fact that he had cut ties with his past in a dramatic way. He was alone, very much alone, as a human being now. A man without a people or family.

"But", he whispered to himself, "the Lord is with me. I trust he will not abandon me as my companions did after the Damascus Road episode." Some twenty or so years later, reflecting back on his early tumultuous experiences after Damascus road he said this: "as servants of God we commend ourselves in every way: in great endurance; in troubles, hardships and distresses; in beatings, imprisonments and riots; in hard work, sleepless nights and hunger; in purity, understanding, patience and kindness; in the Holy Spirit and in sincere love; in truthful speech and in the power of God; with weapons of righteousness in the right hand and in the left; through glory and dishonor, bad report and good report; genuine, yet regarded as impostors; known, yet regarded as unknown; dying, and yet we live on; beaten, and yet not killed; sorrowful, yet always rejoicing; poor, yet making many rich; having nothing, and yet possessing everything" (2 Cor 6:4–10).

---

was a leatherworker and a businessman.

Little did Saul know just how much trouble and distress he would face in the coming years for his newfound faith in Christ. As of this day in Petra, he could not even imagine that within a couple of decades he would characterize his life as follows:

"I have worked much harder, been in prison more frequently, been flogged more severely, and been exposed to death again and again. Five times I received from the Jews the forty lashes minus one. Three times I was beaten with rods, once I was pelted with stones, three times I was shipwrecked, I spent a night and a day in the open sea, I have been constantly on the move. I have been in danger from rivers, in danger from bandits, in danger from my fellow Jews, in danger from Gentiles; in danger in the city, in danger in the country, in danger at sea; and in danger from false believers. I have labored and toiled and have often gone without sleep; I have known hunger and thirst and have often gone without food; I have been cold and naked. Besides everything else, I face daily the pressure of my concern for all the churches. Who is weak, and I do not feel weak?" (2 Cor 11:23–29).

The future was opaque to Saul on this day, and he looked forward to practicing his trade again tomorrow, and making a fresh start in life.

CHAPTER SIX

THE LOVE OF LABOR

THOUGH IT IS TRUE THAT SOME OF THE SOCIAL ELITES IN THE GRECO-Roman world disdained manual labor, and looked down on those who undertook that sort of work,[1] this was not true of Jews in general, and certainly not of Saul in particular. In fact, Saul loved working with his hands to create useful things, and often thought he was emulating his Maker in this.[2] While tanning hides was considered by some Jews as an unclean profession, one of the first things Saul had concluded after his Damascus Road experience was that if a crucified manual worker[3] named Jesus of Nazareth was the Jewish messiah, then the whole issue of what counted as ritually clean and unclean should be re-evaluated. Indeed, Saul was re-evaluating the whole notion that the new covenant Jesus spoke of at his last supper was just a renewal of the Mosaic covenant. Hadn't Jeremiah said that the new covenant would *not* be like the old written code, and would be written on the human hearts, not on tablets of stone?[4]

Saul unrolled his leather tool kit, which was in some ways unique. He used awls made of bone, and yes a knife, a needle, and a pair of primitive scrappers and scissors. Saul did not attempt the sacrificing of the animals, normally goats or sheep, nor did he engage in the tanning of the hides

---

1. See Plutarch, *Per.* 2.1. The funerary inscriptions are clear that tradesmen were often proud of the work they did, and said so on their tombstones.

2. See the analogy he draws about God as a potter in Rom 9:20–21.

3. The Greek word used to describe Jesus' trade is *tekton*, which refers to someone who works in stone or wood, not necessarily a carpenter, but definitely a manual worker.

4. Jer 31:31–33.

themselves. His area of expertise was in producing the finished products from the tanned and cut hides. In the case of making tents, the residents of Cilicia, such as Saul's family, had learned that it was better to leave as much of the goat's hair on the hide as possible, which made it even more waterproof. *Cilicium* was famous around the Mediterranean for being the very best tents one could buy, and they brought a good price.

It is interesting that the Greek phrase "working with one's hands" (1 Cor 4:12; Eph 4:28) or "the work of one's hands" (Acts 7:41; Heb 1:10; 2.7) seem to have been coined by Jews proud of their work and products (cf. Deut 2:7–8; Job 1:10; Ps 89:17; Isa 2:8–9; Jer 1:16–17).

Saul had learned his trade from his father when he was only six years of age, and was a master craftsman by his mid-teens. Alexander had no idea how skilled the man was who had walked into his shop the day before, but he was about to find out. Little did Saul know that Abram had put in a good word for Saul as he bought a few things from Alexander to take back to Damascus and sell. The shop set up in the front of the cave was chilly inside, but at least there was protection from the winter wind and rain which tended to move swiftly through the narrow passage ways in Petra. Sometimes, there would even be flash floods that raced downhill into the market area.[5]

"There is a work bench towards the back of the cave, over there with plenty of light from the hanging lamps. What I'd like you to start with is making some wineskins, one of our best sellers, especially to the winery just across the market square. The smaller squares of leather are over there on top of that amphora. Have a go, and if you have any questions, I'm running the sales end of things from the front of the shop. I'll check back with you later in the morning." On this morning at least, there were only these two men working in the shop.

"Excellent," replied Saul, "I'll get right to work." Saul enjoyed getting back to a trade he had long practiced. Like many another Jew, he believed that God himself in Genesis (Gen 1; Gen 3:17–19) had mandated and validated work as a good activity for human beings created in the image of the Creator, who loved making things. It was not work that was the curse, but rather the toilsomeness of work, and a Jew was apt to recite proverbs about the sin of laziness or indolence (Prov 10:4—the stock figure of the sluggard). And there was one further reason to work—Saul had no desire to become a client of some wealthy patron, neither a parasite or a sycophant.

---

5. Still unto today this happens. See "Jordan rains and floods kill 12, force tourists to flee Petra": https://www.youtube.com/watch?v=IVwQtFWo1gE&vl=en.

PAUL OF ARABIA

At this point in his life he wanted no entangling alliances. He would take Abram's advice to heart—work hard, keep his head down, live quietly, and avoid inequitable relationships.

About two hours into the morning a woman with a head-covering came to the shop to purchase some small items. Saul glanced up and saw her, paying little attention since Alexander was talking to her, but then Alexander said, "Saul, can you come here for a moment?" Saul got up from his stool and came to the mouth of the cave.

"This woman is named Miryam, she is a Jewess from Babylon who moved here some years ago.[6] She sells precious stones and jewelry, and Petra always has a market for such products. She is one of the very few Jewish residents here in Petra and I thought you might want to meet her."

"Shalom," said Saul, "it's good to know I'm not the only Jew in town."

"No, there are a few of us, but even amongst the few, the men tend to be traveling merchants who come and go a great deal. As for me, I stay put and polish stones and make jewelry."

"If I may ask, are you from Babylon originally?" asked Saul.

"Yes indeed, my family did not return from exile but continued to live there as the Persian empire rose and fell, and then came Alexander, and the city became quite Hellenized. My parents spoke Aramaic, but not as their main tongue, unlike my great grandmother who only spoke that language. My generation speaks mainly Greek, and you?"

"I'm originally from Tarsus, but my family moved to Jerusalem when I was a young man, and I studied there among the Pharisees to be a scribe and a teacher. More recently I came here from Damascus, looking for work. Times are rather hard in Damascus just now due to the famine."

"Yes, it has hit the whole region rather hard, and in such times, selling things to make a living becomes more difficult. Well, it is nice meeting you Saul, should you need some jewelry to send to your family members back home in Jerusalem, come see me. My shop is further down the way, near the entrance to the steep steps leading up to al Deir. Alechem shalom."

Saul nodded. Miryam was a woman in her thirties, and when she had left Saul asked Alexander, "Is she not married?"

"She *was* married, but her husband was killed by bandits when he was off to the south to the port of Aela, on the Red Sea. It took a long time for

---

6. Miryam was, in Saul's day, perhaps the most popular of female names, and in fact most of the "Marys" in the New Testament are in fact probably Miryams, named after the prophetess and sister of Moses, though some may have been Marias.

Miryam to find out what had happened to her husband. They were newly married and, perhaps fortunately, had no children yet, but at least she has a trade by which she can support herself. I feel badly for her, but she seems to have persevered through it all."

Saul could not help noticing that Miryam was an attractive woman, and this set his thoughts whirring. He had been engaged as a Pharisee in Jerusalem, but those ties were ended abruptly when the family of the bride learned Saul had become something of a heretic in Damascus. He muttered to himself, "probably best not to think of such things."

"What did you say?" asked Alexander.

"Oh nothing, nothing important. Back to work," said Saul, but clearly his mind was turning over this new development. Would Jesus want him, like the disciples in Judea, to be a married man? He had not considered that possibility since his Damascus Road experience.

Work and Status

Jobs matter and work determined much of one's status in the ancient world. Like today, jobs tended to indicate some level of social prominence or honor. But what positions mattered in the ancient world? The position with the highest social status was the emperor. The emperor carried the most honorable role in all of ancient Roman society. This was a result of not just monetary means (although it certainly included that), but also power, status, and honor. But what about the rest of the 99.9 percent of the ancient world?

Labor is laborious. Such a phrase reveals the ancient mindset that labor itself was looked down upon by those of higher social status.[7] The ability to not "work" or "labor" was prized above the alternative. Underlying a Roman understanding of work and labor was the general notion that those of high status looked down on working with one's hands. More important was the "work of the mind" or work involving rhetoric, politics, or philosophy. One crucial element not to miss is that the Roman world was an empire built on slavery, so much of the work was done by slaves. The attachment of work to slavery may also give insight into the elites' adverse attitudes to work. This Roman attitude strikes against the valuable role that work played within the Hebrew Scriptures where work has a purpose, value, and part of what it means to be human.

---

7. *OCD*, 809.

Where Did People Work?

Ancient cities across the Mediterranean were built around a central market (*agora* in Greek, *forum* in Latin). Shops would line these marketplaces, and most work was done in workshops or small businesses. Craft workers of various physical materials were quite common: working with stone, pottery, glass, leather, textiles, or wood. These craft persons would sell their goods mostly in local markets to various buyers. The ancient world was not a world of mass production, and so these technological liabilities affected the scope of work and localized much work and trade. The more skilled the labor needed, the more status or regard for the person making the product. On top of the social order would be landowning citizens who were among the elite class of the ancient world. They would enlist labor to work their farms for the production of ancient "must-haves" like wine, olive oil, and grain. The production of Roman jars (*amphorae*) and lamps were the exception and traded on a broader scale. Some elite Jewish groups had a more favorable view of manual labor based loosely on examples from the Old Testament.

Status Formation

Roman status was a complicated matter tied up in three related issues of freedom, citizenship, and household.[8] The most elemental status element was the division of people based on non-slave and slave (Gal 3:28; Col 3:11). One should not divorce economics too far from the discussion, one way or the other. Status was not entirely an economic matter. For example, some slaves were incredibly wealthy and could purchase freedom. Another particular nuance was, of course, the slaves in Caesar's household. Such a person would have been connected with the epicenter of Roman power, and hence status. However, even with wealth and good connections, by Roman Law, marriages between freed persons and slaves had no legal standing. Augustus seems to have wanted to further define the social hierarchy in the first century by introducing marriage laws in 18 BC. These laws provided benefits and penalties related to marriage and social classes.[9]

From this division was the division of people groups on citizenship: Roman citizens and non-Roman. Many privileges came with Roman citizenship such a security in travel, appeals to Rome in judicial cases, and different standards of punishment (see Closer Look on Crime and Punishment). Within Roman citizenship, not all persons were entirely equal. The two essential categories being the honorable (*honestiores*) and the humble (*humiliores*) classes.

---

8. *OCD*, 1441.
9. Kehoe, "Law and Social Formation," 149.

The former group included the senatorial classes, the equestrian orders, other high ranking political and military figures, while the latter made up the rest of society. One's status once free and a Roman citizen was then related directly to one's household and the categories above. Honor and status determined the value of a family as well. At the pinnacle of the status structure of the ancient world was the Roman male connected to a prominent household and cascading down through the honorable members of society.

CHAPTER SEVEN

News From Judea

News came to Petra from both the north and the south by means of traders and caravans. One tended to hear about Egypt, now a Roman province, and about Rome's ambitions to continue expanding the empire. Nabatea however was a rather self-sufficient kingdom due to its control and profiting from trade routes from the south and the east, and King Aretas IV showed no interest in sucking up to the Roman rulers and becoming a client king, unlike the Herods, for whom Aretas had nothing but disdain, bordering on hatred, especially after Antipas had dishonored his daughter by divorcing her in order to marry his brother's wife—What an insult!

The news from Judea was spotty, but Saul learned, through conversations with Alexander and also Miryam that the famine in Egypt had led to food shortages throughout the region, including in Judea. Egypt was the bread basket of the empire and one of the main reasons the Romans had incorporated Egypt into the empire was in order to insure a regular flow of grain, on their massive grain freighters traveling across "Mare Nostrum" ("our sea" as the Romans called it) from Alexandria to Rome.

Emperors from Augustus on had made this a top priority, not least because it was by the dole, by free "bread and circuses" that the Romans sought to keep the plebeians in Rome happy and quiet, while the elites just got richer. Some 98 percent of the wealth in the empire was controlled mainly by the upper 2 percent of the population, specifically, by the Romans, although there were client kings and their extended families who also did well.

It dawned on Saul that this situation must increasingly be putting the squeeze on the Jews in Jerusalem who followed Jesus, because increasingly they were being ostracized, jailed, prosecuted, and their widows not allowed to participate in the dole in Jerusalem.[1]

As of yet, Saul had not found time or opportunity to start sharing the good news about Jesus with anyone, but he figured that he did not need to force the issue. Taking Abram's advice, he waited for the Lord to open doors and show him his opportunities.

Alexander had been more than satisfied with Saul's skilled workmanship in the first couple of weeks in his employement, and he had made an arrangement to pay Saul per the number of finished items at the end of each week, as an incentive for him to work hard, though Saul needed no such incentives. He was enjoying his new occupation, and was thinking that if indeed he began to become a traveling herald for the gospel, he would make it a regular practice to continue to ply his trade as he went from town to town. One thing had become clear to him—his would need to be an urban strategy if he was to reach as many non-Jews as possible with the message about a crucified and risen Savior.

Saul also realized that humanly speaking, his message was a hard sell for both Jew and Gentile. Though he had studied the Torah in detail, including the prophets and especially Isaiah, like other early Jews, he had not been looking for a crucified messiah, indeed that whole notion would seem to be a contradiction in terms. No one was reading Isaiah to be referring to a suffering, much less a crucified messiah, not least because earlier in those Servant poems it was *Israel itself* that was called "my servant."[2]

Furthermore, early Jews remembered the text of Deuteronomy[3] and thought that crucifixion indicated a person was clearly cursed by God, not blessed by or anointed by God. On the surface, this end of Jesus' life would seem to make perfectly clear Jesus could not have been God's messiah. Saul himself had thought this way until he had been confronted by the heavenly Jesus on Damascus road, and came to the realization he was alive and well in the very presence of God, and indeed that God had vindicated him by means of resurrection and ascension into heaven, rather like Enoch or

---

1. See Acts 4–7. As we know, this would continue to be an issue well into the 50s, which is why Paul, writing in his earliest extant letter, Galatians, says he promised James he would remember the poor among the saints in Jerusalem (cf. Gal 2; 2 Cor 8–9; Rom 15). This was to become a major focus of Paul's ministry from about AD 50 until he was taken to Rome in about AD 60.

2. Isa 52–53 does not mention crucifixion. See Witherington, *Isaiah Old and New*.

3. Deut 21:22–23 actually refers to public shaming, like what happened to King Saul—the hanging of a corpse on a tree.

Elijah. Furthermore, Jews were not looking for atonement for sin by means of the execution of a Jew!

And for Gentiles, crucifixion was the "extreme punishment" for the most hardened of criminals who had committed treason against the Emperor or the Empire. Never mind that Greco-Roman persons didn't believe in resurrection from the dead as a form of immortality or the afterlife. This whole message about a crucified and risen Savior, or even a crucified God would seem ridiculous to them. So, Saul had much pondering to do if he was going to figure out how a message with that content, could even be listened to for any length of time, never mind received and believed. There was much to ponder as Saul began to formulate a plan of evangelism. He had not been raised to broadcast his faith and seek to convert people, though Jews would readily welcome those they called God-fearers, Gentiles who had come to believe in the one God of the Bible.

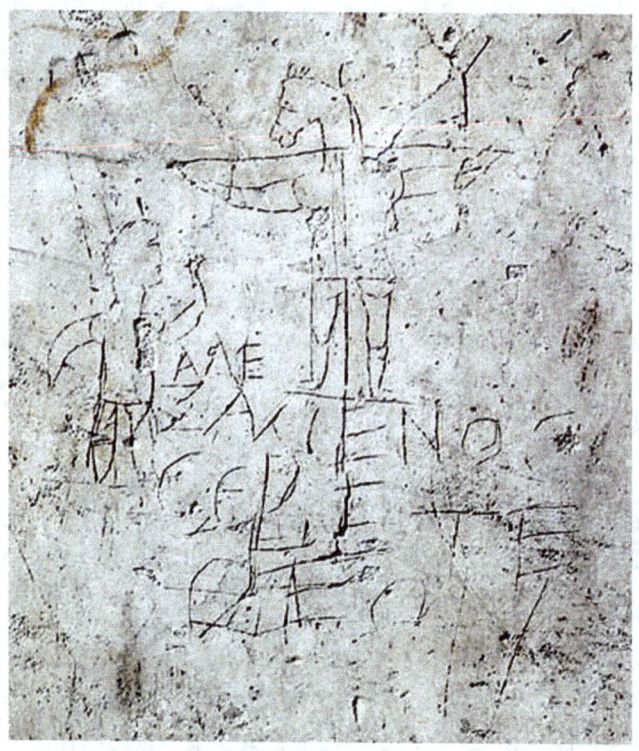

The famous graffito in the Palatine Hill ridiculing the belief in a crucified God. The inscription reads "Alexamenos worships his god," with a donkey being nailed to the cross. In other words, this was seen as an asinine belief.

Today Saul had been tasked with making his first proper tent in many years. It would take several days to accomplish, and he had had to visit the tanner in the village just above Petra to get the right kind of materials. He preferred the hides of black goats, which tended to produce better tents in the long run. The new commission which had come to Alexander had come by way of Aretas' own generals. They needed more tents for their campaigns up north against marauders in general and Herod Antipas' troops in particular.

Suddenly, Saul and Alexander had to make at least ten tents in short order. Alexander had gone out and hired temporarily two other leather workers he knew, plus he brought in his son, Demetrios, who was 22 to help as well. The next two weeks would involve working day and night to fulfill the contract. Saul hardly had time for anything but work, sleep, and eating. In most ways this was a good thing, as it kept his mind off his past, and the things he had lost when he committed himself to Christ.

Jews in the Roman World

It is now the custom when referring to the first century to refer to Judaism(s) plural rather than Judaism singular.[4] There was a radical degree of diversity between various Jewish groups of the first century and hence a monolithic "all Jews" is not historically precise enough to deal adequately with this diversity. We must ask what Jewish groups held which belief, when and what time, and where in terms of location. Alexandrian Jewish groups in Egypt might have unique practices when compared to Jewish groups of Colossae. Essentially we are working against ancient forms of stereotyping. Much of our knowledge of ancient Jewish sects comes from Josephus, Philo, and the New Testament. Perhaps the largest group of ancient Jews were unaffiliated, the *Am Ha-Aretz* or people of the land—peasant farmers, artisans, and tradesmen. Most early Jews probably went about their day unconcerned with the aims and desires of the more specific sects of ancient Judaism.

The main groups in the first century appear to be the Pharisees, Sadducees, the Essenes, and revolutionary groups. Each group has overlapping shared beliefs and unique aspects that made them distinct from the other groups. A small illustration may help. Today, if we asked "what do all Christians believe" there would be some important answers, such as Jesus is the Son of God or the resurrection. If one failed to believe elements like these, one would fail to be Christian (in an Orthodox sense). However, there are many

---

4. Sanders, *Paul and Palestinian Judaism*.

issues that Christians disagree on. For example, if someone wondered what Christians believe about baptism or the Eucharist, there would have to be an explanation of the various views. Holding one of the various views would not place one outside the Christian camp. There would be an allowable diversity within the Christian movement. Not to press an analogy too far, but ancient Judaism is in some ways similar to this modern form of denominationalism (obvious differences exist!). There appear to be a minimum number of issues that hold all of the Jewish groups together. These appear to be monotheism, election, Torah, and temple.[5] For example, if someone wanted to worship idols alongside Yahweh (in terms of actual ideology, perhaps more so than practice), more the merrier but one would cease to be Jewish. It appears the items above are the common thread holding the various groups together. Even a group like the Essenes at Qumran who think the temple is corrupted in the first century, don't negate the importance of the temple as a symbol of ancient Israel.

The Pharisees

The group we perhaps know the most about are the Pharisees. Josephus provides us with much information about their movement. According to Josephus, the Pharisees number about 6,000. Paul, likewise, was an up and coming Pharisee himself. The Pharisees were known for their interpretation of the Hebrew scriptures. They are a table-sect fellowship that takes holiness very seriously. They seem to have taken the Levitical laws for priests and temple and sought to make every Israelite a priest and every home a temple. Why were the extending these holiness laws outward? They were a reform movement within ancient Israel aimed at returning the people to covenant obedience. In a real sense, they are following (a) plotline of the Old Testament. At the end of Deuteronomy, Moses instructs the people that when they find themselves in exile, the way out would be to repent and "return" to covenant obedience. Then Yahweh would gather the people back and return them home and exile would be over. Although the theme of exile in the New Testament is debated, one must admit that the situation in the first century was less than ideal for any Jewish person.[6] It seems as if the Pharisees understand the playbook that got them into this mess (i.e., Covenant unfaithfulness) and are now running the play to get them out—or so they thought.

Although the Pharisees unfairly get a bad rap, they ironically are attempting to be the most faithful. To give the benefit of the doubt, the Pharisees are like many Christians today. They deeply care about not only knowing

---

5. Wright, *NTPG*, 224–32.
6. See the recent excellent work on this topic in Scott, *Exile*.

scripture but faithfully living it out. Of course, that isn't to say that one can have good intentions with bad execution. Good intentions can be distorted and ultimately cause more harm than good. There's a word of warning here for us all.

The Pharisees also have their own interpretive traditions concerning the Torah. Not all legislation in the Old Testament is entirely clear. For example, "what constitutes work?" Interpretive traditions are necessary to interpret and apply scripture. This isn't much different than any pastor today trying to help a community live out scripture faithfully. They also believe in the resurrection and avoid table-fellowship with "sinners." Notable Pharisees joined the Jesus movement (John 12:42), including Nicodemus, and eventually Paul.

The Sadducees

The group we know the least about is the Sadducees. One particular problem is that we possess no sources from the Sadducee movement itself. All our information comes from outside sources commenting on the movement. The Sadducees are connected to the temple in Jerusalem and this serves as their power base. They maintain control of the temple apparatus and the sacrifices therein. They also appear to have a working relationship with the Roman Empire. Most famously, their canon is shorter than other Jewish groups as they "observe nothing apart from the Torah" and thus famously reject the concept of the resurrection. Josephus notes that they had the support of wealthy aristocrats in Jerusalem, but in his opinion (as a Pharisee!) did not have an influential role among the people. Like the Pharisees, their origins are in the Maccabean period and they arise as a response to Hellenization. However, with the destruction of the temple in AD 70 they disappear.

The Essenes

One of the most fascinating groups of the Second Temple period is the Essene movement. They are not explicitly mentioned in the New Testament. Their origins are most likely around 152 BC when Jonathan becomes high priest of the temple.[7] During the Maccabean revolt, the Jerusalem temple was defiled by a Greek general named Antiochus Epiphanies IV. He offered pagan worship in the temple. After the Maccabees purified the temple, it restored proper worship, but this was short-lived. Jonathan came back to Jerusalem to retake the temple after its cleansing, but now with political approval of the Greeks. Jonathan was a political leader and not only was crowned king but

---

7. Ferguson, *Backgrounds*, 522.

also took over the temple priesthood. It's this violation that drives out the old priests who fled to the Dead Sea and most likely formed the community who produced the Dead Sea Scrolls. They see this as a violation of kingly/priestly roles. In their view, the temple has been corrupted as has much of Jewish leadership of the day.

Although according to Josephus they still maintained contact with the temple, and at various points still seem to participate in the temple apparently for prayer and teaching (*J.W.* 1.78–80; 2.111–13; *Ant.* 18.19). The community they form at the Dead Sea produces a vast array of literature. They have internal documents such as communal rules and a war scroll for an eschatological battle between good and evil, along with many copies of scripture. These of course are known as the Dead Sea Scrolls and were discovered in 1947. Properly speaking, the Essene movement is an apocalyptic sect. Unique to them is that they are one Jewish group in the first century looking for two messiahs to deliver Israel—one to cleanse the temple (priestly) and one to lead the people (kingly), this is based on their interpretation of Zech 4:14.

Revolutionary Movements

Most controversial in the study of this period are the groups known as the "resistance movements" of the first century. The origins, aims, and expectations of these groups vary widely. Problematic is that they are often lumped together, but are generally are bound together by their resentment for Roman rule in the land. This puts them on the opposite spectrum when compared to the Sadducees. Most famous are the *Sicarri* or dagger men. They were called this for the short sword they carried with them for political assassinations. They appear to be a group that terrorized fellow Jews. They would kidnap and assassinate Jewish leaders and persons who they thought had accommodated too much to Roman power. According to Josephus, controversially, they are the group that helps to destabilize Roman rule in the in the lead up to the Jewish revolt before the destruction of the temple in 70 AD.[8] Another debated group of the resistance movements is the group known as the "Zealots." Again, according to Josephus, they appear to have the main goal of Jewish freedom and probably looked back to the Maccabean revolt for inspiration and theological validation of their program(s). They found foreign domination as entirely unacceptable and only Yahweh could be their king. The controversy over this group stems from the fact that Josephus first mentions them around

---

8. Grabbe, *Judaism*, 501.

the year 68 AD and they appear to be an combination of several resistance movements.[9]

Such a survey of Jewish groups in the first century shows us the radical diversity of the era. It is therefore difficult and perhaps impossible to apply a broad brush stroke to Judaism of the first century. Likewise, the Jesus movement arises amidst this diversity and Paul and the early churches are amidst this diversity as well.

---

9. Grabbe, *Judaism*, 499–500.

CHAPTER EIGHT

TROUBLE IN ZION

The first decade of life as a Christ-follower, if one lived in Jerusalem or somewhere in Judea, had not been easy, to say the least. Peter and John had been dragged before the Sanhedrin after various sermons and some healings as well in Solomon's portico in the temple, and Peter had even been incarcerated and miraculously escaped, after which he left town. The authorities did not like the fact that these Christ-followers were swaying numerous Jews in the city, even some of priestly descent, even some Pharisees. Some of the more elite converts to Christ, Ananias and Sapphira, had been confronted with their duplicity for lying about what they had given to the common fund to support the community, and had died! Then Saul himself had been present at the stoning of Stephen before he took his life-changing journey to Damascus. Once Peter had left town, the brother of Jesus, Jacob[1] had taken over, and faced many internal problems dealing with Aramaic and Greek speaking widows who needed support and sustenance.

As time went on, and Saul reflected back on his life in Judaism prior to the Damascus Road experience, one thing stood out as an atrocious sin—his persecution of the followers of Jesus. Indeed, when Saul reflected on his past life, on the one hand he was prepared to say that in regard to a righteousness that comes from doing the works of the Mosaic Law he was blameless, but in the same breath mention his persecuting of the church.[2]

---

1. All of the so-called Jameses in the New Testament are actually Jacobs, named after the patriarch.

2. Phil 3:6—notice how he juxtaposes his zeal for persecuting the Christian assembly

If there was trouble in Zion for the Christ-followers, Saul was significantly responsible for the outset of their persecution, prosecution, and even in the case of Stephen, execution via vigilante justice.[3] All these things Saul mulled over as he worked and worked and worked in Petra.

One day a man came to the leatherworking shop wanting a cat of nine tails. When asked what he wanted it for, he said he needed to discipline his slaves.

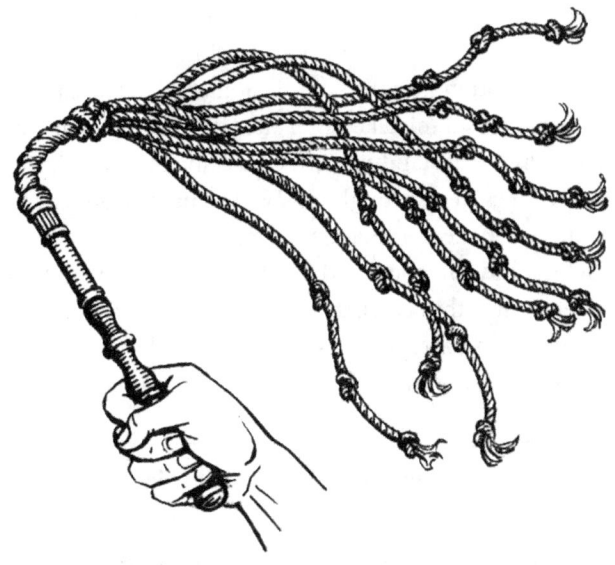

The Roman word is *flagellum* from which we get the word flagellate. It was used as an implement of punishment or discipline, but not of execution.

Alexander headed to the back of the shop to speak to Saul about this, and Saul said in a quiet voice, "I can't in good conscience make one of those that serves no good purpose. It's an instrument of torture, and I have sworn off violence as a means of discipline or torture. I hope you understand. Slavery itself I object to as well."

---

with his blamelessness before the Law. Elsewhere in his earlier and later letters the sense of regret for what he had done to Stephen and others comes through clearly (1 Cor 15:9—"I don't deserve to be called an apostle after doing that"; Gal 1:13; 1 Tim 1:15–16).

3. Jews did not have the right of capital punishment in the province of Judea once the Romans annexed it. They reserved that right to their own governors alone. What was done to Stephen was done against Roman law, not merely without the governor's permission.

Alexander said, "Then we are agreed we'll not make things here that have as their sole purpose harming other people. I myself am a Stoic, and I don't believe in such behavior as a way to solve human problems either. It's sub-human."

"I agree, and when one does such things, it dehumanizes the person doing it as well."

"I'll just tell him we don't make such things in this shop, he'll need to look elsewhere."

The news from Jerusalem continued to be disturbing. More starvation, more Christ-followers fleeing persecution, a process Saul himself had helped set in motion months before.[4] Sometimes, one can only see the enormity of one's sin and mistakes long after the fact. But Saul had come to understand that his right standing with God came through Christ's atoning sacrifice on the cross, not through his own doing of works of the Mosaic law. Saul could not make up or atone for his past sins, but he could accept God's forgiveness and going forward practice the non-violent lifestyle Jesus himself modeled, and that is what Saul had resolved to do. Zeal without understanding of God's mercy and love is not merely misguided, it is misanthropic, a clear sign of human fallenness.

Punishment, Prisons, and Trials

All societies are built on some rule of law and with laws come transgressions and with transgressions comes the need to penalize such conduct. The ancient Roman world was no exception in this regard, but their methods and modes of punishment may surprise us. Rome had a vast legal code with laws governing most aspects of daily life in an empire. What societies criminalize reflect a society's values to some extent or another.[5] What happened when these laws were broken? The first answer depends on an unexpected issue—what's your status? The issues of honor and shame shaped the discourse surrounding punishment in the ancient world. One's status as either a citizen, a free person, or a slave was considered when discussing punishment. Slaves often received harsher and more humiliating punishments than free persons and citizens.[6] Naturally in discussing penalties, the nature of the crime and the degree of intention by the perpetrator.

---

4. Acts 8:1–3.
5. See the helpful article by Reiss, "Roman Bandit," 149.
6. *OCD*, 1278.

How were crimes prosecuted?

Prosecuting an offense was largely a personal endeavor as Rome did not have a public prosecutorial office. The enforcing of laws was the responsibility of the person seeking justice or members of their family. The claim, known as a *delatio* or formal accusation, would be filed with a governor that oversaw judicial issues known as a *proconsul* in the provinces and a *praetor* in Rome. It was the job of the governor to decide whether or not the charge was a civil or criminal matter, and they could easily dismiss cases if they thought the charge was unimportant. If it was a civil matter, the governor could order both parties to court where the case would then be heard by a magistrate or a jury. Such persons usually came from high ranking status, owned land, and were over 25 years of age. Not necessarily a jury of one's peers if one was a non-land owning, low status person. It was up to a magistrate what type of punishment would fit the issue and the fitness of the punishment was often decided on social aspects rather than actual justice. In practical terms, those of lower status could not bring a charge against those of superior rank, and even if it was a possibility, they would not have been able to afford it.

If the action of the charge was criminal the governor would hear the case himself. Often the case would be discussed among a group of his friends known as a *consilium* or the equivalent of legal consultants.[7] Like modern law, cases were judged by precedent. Precedent was set through various collections of laws: local laws and statutes, resolutions of the senate, edicts of magistrates, an emperors's edicts, mandates, responses, or instructions, and eventually jurists or experts of law.[8] The fountain head of the Roman legal legacy dated back to a document known as "the Twelve Tables" from 450 BC. If a similar case had been heard and judged before, they could render a similar verdict. If there was no precedent for the crime, he would have to determine the penalty or punishment. Both magistrates and governors had immense power, or *imperium*, whereby they were accountable for their verdicts only to the senate and the emperor.

One final note, those prosecuting and defending various persons were not lawyers in the formal sense, but rhetoricians using forensic rhetoric. The art of speaking well could be a matter of life and death in a variety of situations. Rhetoric was a political and judicial tool.

---

7. Wansink, "Roman Law and Legal System," 986.
8. Ferguson, *Backgrounds*, 64–65.

What forms of punishment were there?

One's status impacted much of the process. As a general rule, those of honorable status were treated better than those of lower rank. Take example the role of slaves who could be tortured and crucified, not so for the higher status free persons. Capital punishment was usually not for Roman citizens, who were typically banished rather than killed. However, the banishment could be predicated not returning to Rome, lest they face death.[9] Often, they would just remove rights of citizens as punishment which appeared to be rather effective. Banning someone from joining the high rankings of the senate, could dispel their formal punishment. A common type of punishment was flogging, which was mediated on citizens and non-citizens of all status levels. Several different types of financial penalties could also be inflicted and some meant to be disastrous to one's livelihood.[10] One issue that may strike the modern reader as unique is that we have not talked about prisons. Both Greeks and Romans did not practice long-term imprisonment. Often prisons, even ones we see in the New Testament period, were short-term solutions. They were meant to hold someone till trial or for criminals who were waiting for their execution. Prisons were not usually large buildings and even certain rooms in large households could function as a detention room, like we see with Paul at the end of Acts. The only equivalent to our prison system would be a sentencing to the mines, largely a death sentence. The Romans tended to see long-term incarcerations as inhumane. Much better to punish the individual and set them free or sentence them to death if the crime rose to such a punishment.

---

9. *OCD*, 1279.
10. *OCD*, 1279.

CHAPTER NINE

FESTIVAL TIME

SAUL AWOKE WITH A START AS HE HEARD SOMETHING THAT SOUNDED LIKE a trumpet, blowing and blowing and blowing. Hopping out of his bed and throwing on his toga, he peered out of his dwelling into the early morning mist, to see a whole series of shadowy, wildly dressed figures passing by. It was the annual Festival of Atargatis, though Saul did not know it at the time. "That explains why Alexander gave me the day off," said Saul, and he splashed some water from a bowl on his face. Saul flashed back to his younger years when at about the age of ten he had seen such a procession in the city of Tarsus, marching through the Arch of Cleopatra. Ancient religion was bound up with all of ancient social life, including political life, and so it was not entirely surprising that the next thing Saul saw was some exalted figure with a crown on his head, being born by four slaves on a platform.

Standing next to his neighbor, Obadas, he asked, "Is that King Aretas?"

"Yes indeed. They are headed to the great temple built by King Obodas long ago, to sacrifice a bull to Atargatis and petition her for blessings including rain and a fertile spring time."

"But we are in the desert. Do Nabateans grow crops?"

"Mainly no, but there are date palms, and figs, and pomegranates, and all sorts of nuts, and rain is required for those sorts of trees to bear their fruit. Up various of these precipices are flat areas where spring waters collect, and things grow. Aretas even has a stock pond of fish up near al Deir, for the banquets that transpire up there."

Aretas was not a large man, rather he was stocky in build and swarthy in complexion. He had a prominent scar on his left arm, doubtless from one of his battles. Just behind the king came what looked to be priests in colorful garb, chanting and doing some sort of ritual dance periodically.

"Is it permitted to follow the procession and see what happens at the temple?" asked Saul.

"Oh absolutely, this is one of the high holy days in Petra, and the whole town, or almost the whole town comes out to watch, and usually to feast after the sacrifice."

Saul followed along, trailing the priests mingling with the crowd, some of whom were singing a song in a language Saul did not know. At the entrance way to the great temple, the whole procession stopped. A man who appeared to be a high priest turned his eyes towards the heavens and lifted up his hands, and the crowd suddenly became hushed. He invoked the blessing of Atargatis on allthese proceedings. Holding up his knife, shaped like a scimitar he proceeded to the altar in front of the temple where the bull was being held tightly by six strong men.

While this was going on female priestesses had gone into the temple to do reverence to Atargatis and beseech her for her blessings of fertility. Saul did not go into the temple, but he peered through the columns on the side of the temple and could see women kneeling in supplication. "Women priestesses," he whispered. "Well, I guess that explains why so many women are involved in these non-Jewish religions. They have important roles to play."

King Aretas stood outside at the altar as the priest slit the bull's throat, and at once the animal bellowed and then collapsed.

"They drugged the animal first you see so there wouldn't be much resistance," said Obadas.

Saul just nodded, fascinated by this whole ritual. "How many days will the festival go on?"

"Actually, unlike many religious celebrations this is just a one-day festival, on the Ides of Mars." Obadas spoke excellent Greek so Saul had no trouble understanding him.

"Will Aretas, and the priests process up to al Deir for the dinner?"

"Yes, of course, and the drinking symposium will follow, and go well into the night. They say that the symposium speaker this time is some Persian wise man or Magi. It should be interesting as he will talk about what the star beings, the heavenly hosts, have in store for us all in the coming year. But of course ordinary working folk like you and me are not invited. At best, we will find some of the left-over meat for sale over at the *macellum* in the marketplace. A few of the city officials not invited to the dinner at al Deir will have their own feast at the Lion *triclinium* which is only a short way up the same mountain where al Deir is."[1]

---

1. In an age before refrigeration, meat from sacrifices had to be cooked and eaten not long after the sacrifice. Every major city in the Mediterranean had a meat market, but the ordinary person would normally only eat meat during holidays like during this Festival of Atargatis. The word *triclinium* comes from the arranging of three dining couches in an open-ended square with tables for food in the middle.

These are pictures of what remains of the Lion Triclinium at Petra.

"Well, perhaps," said Saul, "you and I could buy some cooked meat at the market and have our own little *convivium* as neighbors. I'm happy to buy the meat, if you and your good wife will provide the rest.²

"Excellent plan. While they will celebrate without us, we will have our own libations and meal."

On the whole Saul was happy with the way things were progressing in his new life in Petra, but still nagging at him was the fact he had not yet found a good opportunity to share his faith. Indeed, it would be some six months before any promising occasion would arise. As far as the people back in Jerusalem were concerned, Saul seemed to have disappeared into the desert sands, for which outcome many Christ-followers were truly thankful.

Entertainment in the Ancient World—Check

Are you not entertained? What did the ancients do for fun? Entertainment took several forms in the ancient world. These ranged from the plays in the theater, the reading of speeches and poetry, to musical performances. The theater of course was the ancient equivalent of the movie theater; dramatic and comedic plays would draw in the masses looking for an evening of leisure. The arenas that dominated the Roman landscape also provided the equivalent of the ancient sport stadium where competition dominated. Further in various cities across the empire would be festivals. Geographic local would determine, just who and what was celebrated, so we ought to expect variations.

Theater: The Roman theater world was highly indebted to Greek theater as its predecessor. The first theater built in ancient Rome is attributed to Pompey in 55 BC.³ Greek theater was performed in the open air and sometimes with a pit for an orchestra. The Roman adaptation modified this open-air structure by adding a *skene* or backdrop at the back of the stage which were often elaborately decorated. One practical aspect of a theater is that it was often the largest place in any city for a public gathering. This made them important places within a city for announcements or important decisions (see Acts 18). Theaters could be adapted for other entertainment purposes as well. Artists, actors, and playwrights would travel from city to city performing various skits and plays. Like movies today, everyday life was depicted, comedy was popular, and satire often dominated the topics as well. The theater was a relief from the

---

2. A *convivium* was a small private dining party, as opposed to a *depna* which was the word for a major feast, usually religious in character.

3. OCD, 1494.

harder aspects of the ancient world. Herod the Great was the first to introduce games and theaters to the Roman East and revolutionized entertainment in the Jewish world.[4] He constructed theaters in Jerusalem, Jericho, and Caesarea.

Religious and social customs also dominated the theatrical world. The patron deity of the arts was the god Dionysius and theaters could be designed to reflect temples and even have altars to gods.[5] Likewise, social customs also dominated this aspect of life. Class and status were on display in attending the theater. Augustus had issued the *lex iulia theatralis* and this divided attendee seating to numerous entertainment events by status such as free to slave; soldier and civilian; to class such as senators and plebs, to gender and even marital status.[6] Colors of clothing would mark out the attendees' social status.

Athletics: Sport was also incredibly popular in the ancient world. Athletic competitions were a form of entertainment dating back to the most famous of athletic events, the Greek Olympics. Sport and physical performance was highly prized by Greeks. One of the most important Greek buildings was the gymnasium that provided a place for exercise and socializing. Greeks would exercise and compete in the nude which was an affront to both Jewish and Roman audiences. In the Roman period, chariot racing and various ball-oriented games dominated the favorite sports.[7] Such competitions were held in the Campus Martia area of Rome or in various circuses (or amphitheaters). Circuses or oval amphitheaters were arenas for chariot racing and the most famous in Rome was the Circus Maximus. Numerous circuses are found outside Rome as well. Various running events would also be held in these arenas. These events were quite popular and many emperors participated and won such events. Although the term "win" should be qualified, who really wanted to beat the emperor?

One of the most famous Roman amphitheaters of the late first century was of course the Colosseum undertaken by Vespasian and expanded by Titus. The Colosseum was built on the former site of Nero's grand palace and henceforth now dominates the landscape of Rome as much now as it did then. The size of the Colosseum permitted not only plays, but large-scale shows, and even was flooded at points to portray famous sea battles. The Colosseum was also of course famous for gladiatorial combats. These spectacles could be either person against person, or person against animal, or just animal fighting. Smaller venues are found throughout the Roman empire. Gladiatorial combat

---

4. Weiss, "Theaters, Hippodromes," 623.
5. Ferguson, *Backgrounds*, 99.
6. Coleman, "Public Entertainments," 339.
7. *OCD*, 207.

actual predates the Roman period. One of the largest gladiatorial combats, before the Colosseum was built, was under the reign of Augustus where 5,000 pairs of gladiators fought in eight games.[8] Just as there are different types of athletes today, there were different types of gladiators. There were professional schools for where one could train to be a professional gladiator; although, this was not considered to be an honorable profession, so much that Augustus and Tiberius banned the senatorial and equestrian classes from becoming gladiators.[9] Professional gladiators were the modern equivalent of all-star athletes. At a simple level, those forced to fight were often simply prisoners of war or criminals. Contrary to popular opinion, not all gladiatorial games were fights to the death. For those who owned gladiators, they had invested considerable resources in training and to kill them would also be to lose valuable income. This of course is to not downplay the violence of the events themselves which many noted and eventually in the late empire were banned as early as AD 325.

Festivals and Games: *Ludi* or games were often associated with festivals. These could refer to fun activities that accompanied religious festivals as well as professional or amateur games. In the early first century there were approx 77 *ludi* days.[10] General leisure activity ranged from wrestling, to ball games, to running. Simple games such as various board games, toys, or dice also were frequently played. Festivals run by the empire required the suspending of business activity, the closing of courts, and some agricultural work was suspended.[11] Festivals honored the gods, the establishing of cities, important military battles, and even military triumphs. The Romans loved to be entertained and their activities and buildings reflect such a desire and aspect of ancient life. Entertainment facilities came to dominate the landscape of ancient Rome and still are some of the most striking architecture of Roman cities.

---

8. *OCD*, 637. See also *Res Gesta* 22.1.
9. *OCD*, 638.
10. *OCD*, 891.
11. *OCD*, 593.

CHAPTER TEN

THE JEWELS OF PETRA

Petra was known for many things, not the least of which was its precious stones which were mined from the rocks and streams in and around Petra and turned into jewelry of various sorts. Having finished work for the day, Saul decided to visit Miryam's jewelry shop and see what she had for sale. It had been several months since Saul had first met her, but he could not get her lovely image out of his mind, so he decided it was time for a visit to her shop. After all, they had much in common, being resident alien Jews in Petra who had a craft.

When he first arrived at the shop she was in the back serving a customer and so he browsed the counter, set out at the front of the cave where she displayed some of her handiwork and he was duly impressed. There was a tray of precious stones carefully polished which one could buy outright, or have put into a necklace, or earrings, or a bracelet, or a ring. Then there were finished pieces, some of which were quite stunning in their craftsmanship.

After Paul had been browsing for about ten minutes, Miryam finally finished haggling with her customer and came to greet Saul.

"Shalom," she said in a soft voice, "it's been some while since we met".

"Indeed. Work, work, work, but after a while even when you love your work, you need a change."

"I couldn't agree more. Did you see any of the Festival last week?"

"I did. Fascinating. I had seen something like it growing up in Tarsus, but living in Jerusalem for the last twenty years as you may imagine, nothing like that happens there, at least not with the involvement of women priestesses."

"Do you object to women in such roles?"

"I used to, but I'm a different sort of Jew these days. I believe we live in a new era, the era of the new covenant Jeremiah talked about, the era when, as Joel says, both men and women will speak God's words of prophecy."

"Interesting. And you don't object to a woman owning her own shop and being a business woman?"

"It seems to me that's a nice fulfillment of what the end of the book of Proverbs talks about when it describes a good wife.[1] So, tell me the story of how you and your husband came to take up permanent residence here, in this very non-Jewish place."

"Well, it's a long story. Do you have time? As long as no customers come along while we talk, I will tell you. But let me first ask—were you looking for something in my shop?"

"Yes, in fact I was thinking of getting something for my sister who lives in Jerusalem. I particularly liked that bracelet. Not too showy but still very elegant and finely crafted."

"Excellent, we can discuss price in due course, but first my story. My husband and I moved from Babylon to here for business reasons. While there is a good trade in garments made of silk on that part of the silk road that heads east and west, my husband's trade was processing fish and making *garum*,[2] that wonderful relish you can put on anything and everything and make it better."

"Wait a minute," said Saul, "There are no large lakes or seas right around here."

"No, you are right," smiled Miryam, "but you'd be surprised how rapidly one can ride a camel to the port of Aela on the Red Sea and come back. Jacob my husband could do it in three days, and he would put the fish in large wineskins, with sea water in them, and then when he got here, dump them in the fishing pond he created up the hill from here. In fact, he's the one who stocked King Aretas' pond up near al Deir."

"So where was his pickling operation? Also up the hill?"

"You have guessed right. And as for me, Petra was a natural source for the sort of gems I love to work with, and just as good a customer base for

---

1. See Prov 31.

2. *Garum* is pickled fish, either sardines, or minced up larger fish and pickled for a considerable period of time. It was extremely popular all over the Mediterraean, as is shone by the large fish pickling industry recently discovered at Magdala by the Sea of Galilee.

my products. You'd be surprised how many elite people of many tribes and nations pass through or visit Petra. It is no backwater place."

"Yes, that thought had begun to dawn on me. So how long have you lived here?"

"Before I answer that, would you care for a cup of good wine?"

"Absolutely. The air here is so dry I find myself often parched. I've even taken to drinking some of the spring water, which can be refreshing at times, but not as flavorful as the wine of course."

"No, indeed. Here you go. This is the finest our town winery has to offer."

"Ummmm . . . that's really excellent, not bitter at all." Saul was enjoying this conversation and did not want it to end.

"So you moved here when?"

"Almost three years ago. It seems a very long time ago now. But it must be that long for it's been a year since my husband was found dead an hour away from here in the desert on the road back from Aela—bandits!"

"I'm very sorry," said Saul, "I too lost my intended one, because I joined a group of Jews that the family of my betrothed despised and called heretics. But your loss is clearly much greater than mine."

As the conversation was drawing to a close, Saul asked, "So what would you consider a fair price for that bracelet?"

"For my fellow Jew Saul, a special price—two days' wages."

"Surely it is worth much more than that!" exclaimed Saul.

"Well yes, but let me honor your sister. What is her name?"

"Deborah."

"Excellent. I will carve her name in Hebrew in the filigree of the bracelet and make it personal. You can come back and get this in a couple of days."

"I will certainly do so. It's been a pleasure making your acquaintance, and I would like to continue our conversations at some convenient time in the not-too-distant future."

"And I would like that as well," smiled Miryam. "Shalom. See you soon."

"And alechem shalom as well."

Things had gone well in this first real conversation, and Saul was hoping this was only the beginning. After all, the Lord himself had said it was OK to marry if the God of the Bible brought those two people together and joined them as one.

CHAPTER ELEVEN

THE KING'S SPEECH

It was a custom of Aretas IV to address the people in his capital city once a year, and normally the speech would come on the first day of the month the Romans named for Juno, and this year was no different. It had been exceedingly hot in Petra already for over a month, and the temperature on speech day could only be called blisteringly hot. While the loyal Nabateans enjoyed an occasion to gather, not least because Aretas normally would give gifts of wine and bread on the occasion to all those present, on this day, they were looking for some shade, and there was none to be had because Aretas chose to give the speech from the highest point in the city, in front of the ancient necropolis up on the hill, and in order to hear the king one had to stand in the sand below the precipice.

"Let us hope the king is in a merciful mood today," said Obadas to Saul, "and does not speak overly long."

"Abandon hope," replied Saul, "this king likes to hear himself talk, and you will notice that they have placed his throne in the shade up there while we bake in the sun." Obadas simply groaned.

"Look, his slaves have brought palm leaves to fan the king with. This does not augur well for our being dismissed in time for an early mid-day meal."

"Alas, you are too right," replied Saul, "we are in for a long siege. Fortunately I brought a piece of sturdy papyrus to fan us with."

The state of the kingdom speech began with a flourish of trumpets, which resounded off the walls of the necropolis, followed by a herald introducing the king by mentioning his twenty-five throne names, of which

Aretas Phillopatris, "the Excellent One, lover of his Country," was just the last.

Fortunately, the king had a good strong voice, and he began his speech with a nice *exordium* about how loyal and trustworthy his subjects had been for many years. He then proceeded to list his many accomplishments of the year, not least of which was the conquering of territory of Herod Antipas east of the Jordan river. He added "Let it be known that Jews like Herod are not to be trusted, not to be believed, not least because they defame our gods, calling them idols or even non-entities. It is a laughable claim. Were Atargatis not with me in battle, fighting on my side, I could not have conquered the land of Perea so easily against superior forces."

Saul whispered to Obadas, "the king does not seem to know that the Herods are as much Idumean as Jew, and that originally they came from this side of the Jordan, for an Idumean is nothing more than the most recent name for the Edomites, often the enemies of the Jews of Judea."

Obadas grinned and said, "Perhaps you should seek an audience with the good king and better educate him on the matter."

"After that comment the king just made, that would be exceedingly foolish. I can see the scene now. 'Greetings your majesty I'm a Jew who believes in only one God and it's not Atargatis, I thought I'd correct a few of your errors in your recent speech.' That would probably be the last time I spoke to anyone!"

"I was only joking," said Obadas.

The speech droned on for two more hours, as Aretas proceeded to read out the list of booty his troops had taken from the Galilean king and his minions, and just when one thought he was wrapping things up, having said "and finally" he went on for five more minutes, explaining how now he had not only cleared the trade route all the way to Damascus of all bandits and thieves, but that he had in fact taken control of the territory all the way up to and including Damascus in the last year.

By the time the speech was over, two hours after it began, every one standing below was soaking wet under their robes and togas, and dying of thirst. Only then did the herald blow the trumpet again and one could see in the distance a line of camels coming carrying huge wineskins. Each citizen of Petra was expected to bring their own drinking vessels, but Saul did not know this was the custom.

"Not to worry," said Obadas, "I brought two so we could slake our thirst together."

THE KING'S SPEECH

"Thank goodness for friends! I am parched."

The two men, having gotten their allotment of wine and bread, retreated to the comfort of Obadas' cave.

"Why did we not see Aretas' queen?"

"Oh, you mean Shakilat. Well, she is on the coins, but she does not much appear in public. The rumor is the sun burns her. Her skin you see is fairer than many here."

"So, she is not a native Nabatean?"

"No, I believe she is ultimately from Persia, and she has fair skin and light-colored hair and eyes. You know how these rulers are. They marry other king's daughters to firm up alliances with neighboring rulers. Only that didn't turn out well when Herod Antipas jilted Aretas IV's only daughter for one of his own cousins! The people of Petra talked of nothing else for months when they heard about this."

"But Aretas got his swift revenge."

"He did indeed. And since Shakilat is a new wife, perhaps she is with child and could not come out today."

"Well, someday, I do hope to meet your king, God willing," said Saul.

"Well, my advice is, not any time soon, when bad Jews are still on Aretas' mind."

"That's good advice. I will bide my time." The sun had gone down, and tomorrow Saul would be back at work early, so he bid his farewell to his friend, and went back to his lodgings. In his evening prayers he said, "Lord, when will there be an opening for me to share the good news about you with the people and ruler of Petra? This place does not seem to be fertile soil for sowing that seed about your salvation and love. Prompt me to act at a propitious moment when you have opened a door." With these thoughts on his mind, Saul blew out the lamps hanging in his room and lay down until the sun came creeping into his cave, the next morning.

Rhetoric and Education in the Ancient World

What's in a word? Well, just about everything in the ancient world. A word well spoken was revolutionary in Paul's day. The ancient world was a rhetorical world. Generations before, Aristotle had coined rhetoric as "the art of speaking well" and it became a form of social currency. One could ascend social ranks of prestige and influence by speaking well. Although there was no standard education practice—at an empire-wide level—rhetoric was baked in to the educational systems of the ancient world. Even if one could not afford to have advanced rhetorical training, like Paul, many picked up rhetorical skills and practices from the lower levels of education. Even letter writing was a part of early elementary rhetorical training, because these were oral cultures and the letters would be read out loud. Actual letter handbooks come after the New Testament era, whereas rhetorical handbooks had long been in existence before the New Testament age.

Ancient rhetoric was all about persuasion. The three main categories of rhetoric—forensic, deliberative, and epideictic rhetoric—were all aimed at persuading an audience of a particular choice of action. If forensic, one was in the law court, attempting to argue for a right or wrong of something done in the past. This type of rhetoric aimed to achieve justice. We're very familiar with this type of rhetoric as it is the rhetoric of every law-court TV show. We love, just like the ancients, to see a rousing accusal or defense of a person.

Deliberative rhetoric was the rhetoric of future choices for a group, what was in the group's advantage or disadvantage with various decisions. This appears to be Paul's favorite category of rhetoric as many of his letters are deliberative. Much of this makes sense, since Paul is frequently aiming to get his congregations to decide on something important. We're used to this type of rhetoric, we see it every election season. Candidates are attempting to persuade a free-body of citizens to choose them. This cannot and should not be forced, but the persons still need to be persuaded of a course of action.

The last category of rhetoric was epideictic and this was an all encompassing category. Mainly found in a speech of praise of a funeral oration. This species of rhetoric used praise and blame to confirm existing opinions. One has probably heard a epideictic speech when listening to a eulogy.

The ability to work with ancient audiences was largely dependent on the ability to speak well. An ancient person wanting to persuade a group would be more inclined to give them a persuasive speech, rather than an eloquent tome. But didn't Paul write letters? So was he not that bright in sending massive documents to an illiterate audience? While it must be admitted that the "weighty letters of Paul" were not the most effective means of communication, they did meet various needs Paul had. Mainly communication across distance. This was not a large weakness, as Paul wrote his letters to be read aloud to the community. The letters were to function as a stand-in for Paul. To this end, Paul probably worked with and trained his letter readers to read them with the rhetorical flourishes and emphases he desired. For example, in Rom 16:1, we meet a women named Phoebe and Paul "commends" her. The language of commendation came right out of the vocabulary of letter readers and indicates that Phoebe was the first to read and interpret Romans to the Roman congregation.

Paul stands out in the ancient world as a highly literate, highly educated, and highly rhetorical person. His letters evidence the profound ability to speak in rhetorical ways utilizing all the key methods of ancient rhetoric. Indeed, perhaps one of the reasons we are still so captivated by Paul's letters is a testament to his rhetorical ability. Throughout Paul we gain glimpses of both his macro and micro use of the rhetorical traditions. In the micro-scale, one thinks immediately of the famous "I" section of Rom 7 where Paul utilizes the rhetorical practice of "speech in character" to give us a "speech" of some sort in the voice of "Adam." Or maybe you've noticed Paul is a detailed person? When reading Gal 1, and picking up Paul's itinerary and resume, one notices the precision of argument. Such was common for something known as a *narratio* or a narration of the facts. On a macro-level, remember the great passionate defense argument of Rom 9–11, a classic refutation of perceived arguments from one's opponent. In Rom 9–11, Paul is single-handedly slicing through proposed objections to the marvelous masterpiece of Rom 1–8.

CHAPTER TWELVE

THE QUICKENING

After a very hard day's work, finishing up no less than three tents in a single day, Alexander had given Saul permission to leave an hour early to do a little shopping before the market closed down at sunset. In reality, Saul would only spend a few minutes at the market, his real aim was to get to the jewelry shop before it closed. He could not get Miryam out of his mind, try as he might. When he arrived at her shop, she was just clearing the table of her precious stones and jewelry items and looked up and smiled—"Shalom stranger, it has been a while."

"Yes," said Saul, but not by choice. "Alexander has been working me like a dog in order to get his shipment of tents off to the Nabatean army in time. He has worn me out the last few weeks."

"Well, at least you can be thankful you have decent employment, which is more than many can say."

"You are right. I should just be grateful, being an alien here. I stopped by to ask, if you think it appropriate, if we could have dinner together."

Miryam smiled and said coyly, "Are you hoping this may lead somewhere?"

Saul scratched his forehead, "Is it that obvious? Yes, I was hoping we might take some time and get to know each other well, that is if it's not too soon after the period of mourning for your late husband. I noticed you were no longer wearing black and the veil anymore."

"No, it is not too soon, and in truth, I could use some company about now. So I have an idea. There is actually a decent *taberna*[1] down the pas-

---

[1] *Taberna* from which we get the word tavern, was an ancient restaurant and

sage way beyond the entrance to the climb up al Deir hill. Shall we go and see if there is something worth eating there?"

Saul beamed, "It would be my great pleasure," and he held out his arm. "You lead the way." As it turned out, the *taberna* was yet another cave hollowed out into a public place, and this one was beneath yet another necropolis. You could see the doorway into the *taberna* from some distance away.

Notice the cave with the wooden door, which is in fact a restaurant.

The host of the *taberna* was standing at the door welcoming guests.

"This is our host Gandras," said Miryam, "and his wife is a very good cook indeed."

"You grace us with your presence again lady. And who is this lucky person on your arm this evening?"

"This is my friend Saul, and we are starving, so I trust you have plenty of good food to serve this evening."

"But of course. My wife has been cooking most of the day." Gandras escorted the two to a quiet spot just inside the door on the right. There was an impressive lamp on a stand in the middle of the table with multiple spouts. "I will go get some wine and bread to start and be right back."

---

sometimes hostel as well for ordinary people, especially travelers.

When Gandras returned, Miryam said, "What is your soup today that you serve as a first course?"

"Today we have a nice lentil soup which you have sampled before and liked."

"Excellent. Saul, if you are agreeable let's start with two bowls of that good hot soup." Saul simply shook his head yes, impressed with the rapport and charm Miryam had when dealing with a man like Gandras. She knew how to make him feel appreciated.

When the soup had come, Miryam suggested, "Perhaps you could say a blessing for us?"

"Gladly. Gracious God, who brings forth bread from the earth, we give you thanks for what we are about to receive, knowing that ultimately all good gifts come from you. Bless not only the food but our conversation and time together, in your holy name. Amen."

"That was beautiful," said Miryam, "Now, tell me about you, first."

Saul had not had the problem of being tongue-tied in the past, but he found himself groping for the right words. He did not want to say the wrong thing and prevent a real relationship from blossoming.

"As I believe I mentioned before, I grew up in Tarsus, in a devout family. They are devout Jews, Pharisees in fact."

"So they believe in things like angels and resurrection, right?"

"Yes you are correct. We moved to Jerusalem when I was a young man so I could study with the famous Gamaliel and become a scribe and teacher in due course. I thrived in that environment. In fact, Gamaliel said I was his top student, advancing in Judaism beyond my peers. My parents were quite proud of me, and I was very zealous for the traditions of our ancestors and deeply concerned about things that might mislead our people in an already troubling time.[2] This zeal led me to take a harsher approach to those I considered heretical Jews than Gamaliel, who simply said 'if those people following Jesus of Nazareth are wrong and their message is not of God, then it will fail. If it is of God and you trouble them, then you will be opposing God's own will. Leave them alone!' But I was young and headstrong. I did not listen. I thought they were deceivers of the people, and my zeal was so great, that I began to persecute these people, brought them before the Sanhedrin, even stood by when one of them named Stephanos was stoned. And the Sanhedrin sent me to Damascus to drag some more 'heretics' back for trial in Jerusalem. I tell you all this not to frighten you, but to be honest, because a great change came in my life after all that, and I needed to explain what led to it."

"Well, thank you for your honesty, Saul, and I will honestly say, I don't like the sound of all that. I say live and let live."

"You are right, and I learned that to my great cost, but let me explain why and how I am a changed man."

Saul continued, "I'm sure as a good Jew you believe God can and does do miraculous things, and I'm not a person given to claiming that any and every fortuitous event is a direct miracle from God. In fact, I had never seen or experienced an actual miracle before my journey up Damascus Road to take prisoner some Christ-followers. Do you know about that sect of Judaism?"

"I've heard a few things, but not much. Please explain."

"They are people who believe that Jesus of Nazareth, a man born during the time of Herod the Great, and who died by crucifixion at the hands

---

2. See what Paul says about his past in Gal 1.

of Pontius Pilate is the Messiah, and that in fact God raised him from the dead, vindicating his claims to be the Messiah. I must confess that when I heard of this, I laughed at first—whoever heard of a crucified messiah? That's a contradiction in terms. Surely, the anointed of God would not endure the curse of being crucified."

"Yes, that is what I would have thought," said Miryam, "but go on."

"Well, there were all these claims of people said to have seen Jesus alive after crucifixion, and even to have dined with him! Instead of crucifixion putting an end to that sorry far-fetched tale, these claims of his reappearance caused it to spread, rapidly even in Jerusalem, Judea, and all the way to Damascus. I thought something had to be done to put a stop to this incredible tale and its proclaimers. So with a commission from the Sanhedrin I headed out of the city gate on the 100-mile walk up to Damascus with some companions. As we approached Damascus, something inexplicable happened." Just as Saul was about to explain, the soup arrived.

"If nothing else, this is an intriguing story," said Miryam, "but let's take a little pause and enjoy our soup." The soup was indeed delicious, and had some sort of spice in it, perhaps cinnamon which made it even more tasty. In the middle of that course Saul said, "I hope you will share with me your story as well. I am simply trying to be frank from the outset, so you will not be surprised later."

"Well, I always appreciate candor and despise deception, so that's all good, and yes, I will tell you the pertinent parts of my story as well." Gandras was standing nearby and said: "I don't mean to interrupt, but are we ready for the next course?"

"Yes, of course," said Miryam, "what is it this evening?"

"It is lamb shanks cooked in goat's milk with seasonings."

"It sounds delicious," said Miryam. "Bring it on in due course. There is no hurry. For now, we need a bit more bread and olive oil.

"Continue your story," prompted Miryam.

"So I was minding my own business, not expecting divine intervention but not long before we arrived in Damascus I was flattened on the road by a heavenly vision, so bright, so clear, and no it was not just sun stroke or the like. My companions did not see the person I saw in the light or hear the voice I heard, as it was a communication just to me, but they did see the intensification of light and heard some sort of garbled sound, knowing that something dramatic was happening to me."

"Are you saying the God of our Fathers appeared to you?"

"Not exactly. The person who appeared was Jesus of Nazareth, the very person I despised and thought was a false messiah. And he appeared from the right hand of our God! He was not only risen from the dead but exalted to God's right hand as his Son. Please believe me that I was not prepared for this revelation, and had someone shared these notions with me before then, I would have said they had lost their mind. But I could not deny my own direct experience, and this Jesus asked me a very odd question—'Saul, Saul why are you persecuting me?' Notice he did not ask 'Why are you persecuting my followers?' which I was doing. In other words, an attack on them was an attack on this heavenly Jesus, and what Gamaliel had warned me about was coming true—I was actually opposing the will of the God of our ancestors who had raised Jesus from the dead, vindicated his claims, and exalted him to his right hand! This experience left me mentally shattered and groping for answers, and physically I was struck blind. The person who thought he could see through this Jesus hoax, had actually seen the risen Jesus and it completely changed his life, by which I mean my life. I went from being a persecutor of the followers of Jesus to being one of them! I was taken into Damascus by my companions and left at a house of their fellow Jews—blind and badly shaken."

The bread had come, and they both tore off a piece and ate some.

"Please continue," said Miryam.

"Equally unexpected was what happened next. A Jew named Ananias who lived in Damascus, himself had a vision and he was directed to come to me, lay hands on my eyes, baptize me and give me instructions of what God wanted me to do."

"And what did he want then?"

"He wanted me to share the good news about our Savior and Lord Jesus, particularly with non-Jews. Now I knew that I could not go back to Jerusalem at that juncture. I knew I myself would be tried by the Sanhedrin, and it was entirely unlikely that the leaders of the Jesus movement in Jerusalem would receive me either, since I had just been persecuting them! So I resolved to go somewhere else where there were non-Jews. Somewhere rather remote from Jerusalem where I could figure out just what God expected me to do. I've not told you my whole tale. I will just add that I am a single man, formerly betrothed who lost his intended one, when the family found out I'd turned into a Christ-follower. I do not even know if my parents or sister would receive me if I returned to Jerusalem. I was a man without a people, and without a family, and even without a group of fellow worshipers of the one true God, when I came here."

"That's a lot for me to swallow in one gulp, and fortunately our meal is now here. So let me process what you've said, and let's enjoy this good food." And the food was truly delicious. It came with some more bread, but also with a dipping sauce for the bread as well. The two filled their bellies with this excellent meal and were feeling quite satiated when Gandras returned and asked—"Shall I bring some more wine, and the fruit course now?"

"Oh yes please," said Miryam. The fruit that came was bananas, figs, and even a pomegranate. Saul cut the fruit up and they shared it from the same plate.

"So," said Saul slowly, "are you going to tell me I have taken leave of my senses, or must have drunk too much wine along the way to Damascus?"

"No," said Miryam, "but you have to admit, it's a lot to take in. I've never heard a story like that, but then Torah is full of stories about how God comes in a vision or by an angel and changes a person's life. My goodness the story of Ezekiel, which we exiles often told in Babylon, is all about unexpected divine intervention is it not?"

"Yes indeed it is," replied Saul. "I do not claim to have visions every second Sabbath, but I do claim I had this one and it changed my life. . . . And altered its course irrevocably."

"I must ponder your story some more, but as we draw this surprising dinner to a close, a few things about me, and I'll tell you more the next time we have dinner. I am an only child, and my parents and now my husband are gone. I have had no children as well, but not through any choice of my own. I would love to have children of course. It is every good Jewish woman's heart's desire. But it has not happened that way for me. I will be honest and say, I am a devout Jew who believes there is only one God as Torah says. . ."

"As do I," interrupted Saul.

"And I know the prophecies do speak of an anointed figure coming along at some point to save our people, but this Jesus isn't quite what I imagined our messiah would be or do. I expected him to come and kick the Romans out of Judea at least."

"Yes, that's what a lot of Jews had longed for. But this Jesus was not a military leader like David. He was a man of peace, who road into Jerusalem at Passover on a donkey proclaiming the final saving reign of God was at hand, and it did not involve violence, but rather true shalom. Perhaps our

God did not send us the messiah we expected. Perhaps however he sent us the one we needed to redeem our own people."

"In any case," said Miryam, "I am at a crossroads in my life, and do not know where it is leading."

"That's about the truth with me as well. Perhaps God really has brought us together for a time such as this."

"Maybe so, but I will need to pray on all this." The meal was over, and Saul insisted on paying the bill. While he was doing so, Gandras pulled Saul aside and whispered in his ear, "Be good to that woman, she has suffered much, and would be a good match for any good man," to which Saul replied in a whisper. . . "Well, I hope I am good enough."

As Saul had stared through the lamplight at the table at the beautiful olive-skinned woman with deep brown eyes, his heart had beat rapidly, and he knew he was smitten. Walking home with her on his arm he only hoped that his candor had not destroyed his chances with Miryam.

Arriving at her door, she said "Until the next time," and gave Saul a brief hug.

"Until the next time then, shalom," he replied, and he did not intend to let that be too many days from this memorable one.

Dining and Food

Dining is part of the human experience. Although all humans love to eat with one another, they do not eat the same way with one another through time. Eating a meal in the Greco-Roman world was no small affair. What we regard as simply a meal was a social event in the ancient world. In short, the dining experience was a place of social contest. So where, how, and with whom did Romans eat?

Where did they eat?

The Latin word for the dining room is the word *triclinium*, which gives us a clue into the architecture of ancient eating. The *triclinium* initially referred to a three couch arrangement in the shape of an upside down *U*.[3] Usually, a table was set at the end of one of the couches or in the middle of the couches, and those eating could recline on their left elbow and be able to reach the food with their right hand. Guests are referred to in Latin as *convivae* and hence the term for the banquet itself *convivium*. When one thinks of dining like this,

---

3. *OCD*, 469.

one should not think of the average everyday Roman, but of the upper classes who had room for such a dining experience. Many of the poor of ancient urban cities lived in what we today would call high-rise tenement apartments. Dimly lit and under-ventilated, many would choose to spend much of the waking hours of the day outside. The poorest residents could either choose to eat in their less than optimal apartment or venture out into the city to eat at an outdoor venue such as *caupona*, a *popina*, or *taverna*, the equivalent of walk-up food trucks, fast-food restaurants, or taverns.[4] Such places offered food for purchase if one could afford it. As the popularity of public and larger gatherings grew, the triclinium came to refer to much larger groups, sometimes up to twenty tables to a room. Depending on the size of the home, there could be multiple dining rooms, but indoor and outdoor dining was popular depending on the season. Often dining would be combined with some form of entertainment, so larger spaces grew in popularity that allowed for both dining and the public performance of music, art, and literature. Conversation topics at dinner ranged from politics to religion, to world events and economics. Dinner parties could also be moral battlefields as it was frequent for drunkenness to take a turn for the worse and end up in brawls or sexual misconduct. Dancing girls and sometimes even prostitutes made appearances later in the evening.

What did they eat?

One must remember that an abundance of food is a luxury. As we look at the Roman diet, most people lived a subsistence lifestyle, and this did not entail a broad diet. Most ancient persons lived on a diet of grains, beans, olive oil, and wine.[5] Only the rich could afford a diversity of food products in the ancient world. The standard feature of ancient meals was wheat or barley. Often these could be made into a porridge or baked into bread. There was free grain in Rome, so breads must have been plentiful. Lentils, peas, or various beans were how many people gained protein in the ancient world. As part of the Mediterranean world, olive oil was a popular product, and one means to secure fats in a diet. A variety of fruits and vegetables, depending on one's location, were also available for consumption. Although meat is plentiful in today's world, it was a luxury in the ancient world. One can't forget that without refrigeration, it is hard to preserve meat. So, meat became a luxury item in the ancient world and often was associated with religious festivals where animal sacrifice was common. So much food was bound to make one thirsty, so what would ancient people drink? Wine was the most common drink as water might not be the

---

4. Witherington, *Conflict and Community*, 191.
5. *OCD*, 603–4.

safest choice in the ancient world. Meat served at a party would be a sign of status and wealth, and drinking could create a variety of problems depending on how much was consumed. The more rare, exclusive, or novel the food items offered, the more prestige and notoriety the host would gain. Romans typically ate three meals a day. A minimal breakfast, and a medium-sized lunch was common in the first century. The most substantial meal of the day was the evening meal known as the *cena* and came after the typical workday.

With whom did they eat?

Dining in the ancient world inevitably crossed social strata. At a typical meal, everyone from the high-status wealthy donor to the low-status servants were included. A range of statuses in-between dotted the landscape of ancient dining rooms. As such, all the social conventions were equally at play. Several notable ancient authors comment on the treatment of lower status individuals at these meals. Ancient dining often resembled, stepping onto an airplane in the modern world. Where you sit on the plane matters and status and wealth are involved. Those with the means get the best seats on the plane in first class where they get better pillows, better blankets, and more legroom. First-class travelers are served with better food and wine and typically with more exceptional dining utensils. This of course comes at a cost. If one cannot afford the first-class ticket, economy offers new opportunities, but ones that come with a price-tag as well. Sitting in economy, one receives less prioritized seating, no alcohol, and food with less quality than the first-class cabin. It's more crowded, and one wonders if the flight attendants pay less attention. One can easily map our modern experience of airplanes onto the ancient dining experience. Often people of lower classes were served inferior food and wine, set in less auspicious places, and were neglected in comparison to the more influential members of the dinner party. Class and status were at play in the dining world of ancient Rome. Often the one seated closest to the host was the most honored guest. Martial, in his epigrams comments on the stratification that happened at meals, establishing the pecking order: "Since I am asked to dinner . . . why is not the same dinner served to me as to you? You eat oysters fattened in the Lucrine Lake while I suck a mussel through a hole in the shell. You get mushrooms while I get hog fiunguses. You tackle turbot, but I brill. Golden with fat, a turtledove gorges you with its bloated rump, but a magpie that has died in a cage is set before me. Why do I dine without you, Ponticus, even though I dine with you?" (Epigrams 3.60).

Dining in public

Another popular opportunity for eating was in public with feasts often hosted by the emperor himself. Julius Caesar boasted of offering a meal that included over 22,000 *triclinia*. Commonly these events could be used by a variety of politicians to secure the goodwill of the people or just for good public relations, although Roman law tried to regulate meals for such purposes. A wealthy donor could increase their honor by showing their generosity in public by throwing a free dinner in the municipal center for a wide variety of guests. Such meals often accompanied a victory, the dedication of a building, or even the death of a beloved resident. It is difficult to draw lines between public and private banquets as such distinctions were hard to maintain in the ancient world. A variety of groups met for shared meals in the ancient world. These groups, known as *collegia* or associations, included everything from religious groups to businesses to local unions of a particular trade. These groups brought together by a common cause, would typically have a meal in the context of their business meetings or religious gatherings. The early Christians partook of this common ancient practice. Notably for the early Christians, crossing the social classes created both unique opportunities and challenges for various communities. The questions facing these gatherings would involve asking what social scripts would be in operation at the early Christian meal. Was it "business as usual"? Or would the story of Jesus come to have a radical effect on the dining practices of these early Christian groups?

CHAPTER THIRTEEN

THE JOURNEY TO AELA

Alexander was understandably having an anxiety attack. The king had given him a mandate to get those ten tents to Aela within the week, and he had been unable to track down his camel-driving courier to do the job. And the deadline was only four days away. Finally, he asked Saul—"Will you go then? I'll provide the two camels, one to carry the goods and one for you, and I have a map here somewhere to guide you."

Not knowing the road, or the circumstances, Saul was reluctant to say yes, but he could see Alexander was in a huge bind so instead he said, "Of course I will go. I'll leave as soon as you've packed the camels."

And so, unexpectedly Saul found himself taking a business trip to the seaport on the Red Sea nearest Petra. Aela was in fact on the very tip of the gulf and Saul would have to go through Humema, an oasis, in order to get there. He could reach the oasis by late afternoon if he hurried. The first part of the journey proved to be easy. Saul's camel was named Jai and the other camel was tethered to him. Jai knew how to move quickly and smoothly in the desert, and before twilight Saul saw Humema on the horizon—Saul resolved to make a quick night of it, and be up at dawn in order to get to Aela. When morning dawned, what he had not counted on was an ornery camel that did not like getting up early! Finally, taking the advice of another business man at the oasis, he got Jai and his companion some "camel treats" and suddenly, they were ready to move! It took the rest of the day to get to the Nabatean camp at Aela, and Saul made it barely before complete darkness descended.

The contact person he was to meet at the Nabatean came was named General Rubalel. Fortunately, the general had an interpreter fluent in Greek. Saul handed over the much needed tents, had a little supper, and planned to head straight back to Petra, but there was a problem. The general had warned that they were expecting a sand storm, a *hamsin*, sometime soon, perhaps as early as the morning. Saul thanked the general for the heads up, and decided he would wait and see the conditions before he departed the camp.

Aela proved to be a town larger than what Saul had expected. When he arose the next morning, sure enough hot winds were blowing off the desert toward the sea, and Saul delayed departure to see what would happen next. He went down to the water front and watched small and large boats unloading their cargo. Most of the boats had come across the Sea from Egypt, as one could tell from their distinctive design.

THE JOURNEY TO AELA

Mainly they were off-loading fish, but there was one boat that was taking off bundles of spices, and even some perfume. Saul recognized one of the labels which said "pistic nard."[1] Saul couldn't resist purchasing a very small vial of it for Miryam. He hoped she liked it.

By afternoon, Saul notice a train of camels mounting up to head north to Petra, and Saul asked the camel driver if he could tag along. "Will you be going back by Humema and then up to Petra?"

Hakan said he would, and would welcome the company. There was safety in numbers after all. The caravan reached Humema by dark, and Saul reckoned that he would be able to get back to Petra by mid-day the next day. All in all, the trip had gone about as well as it could, up to that point.

The next morning dawned, and when Saul awoke, somehow the caravan had already slipped away, but he reasoned he was only a few hours now from Petra so he was not greatly troubled. He saddled up Jai and his companion, and after eating a piece of bread from his saddle bag he set off. The problem with the desert, of course, is that everything looks the same in all directions, and it is all too easy to get lost. After a few false starts and wrong turns, he got lucky—a large train of camels came along heading up the Spice Road, and Saul simply tagged along with them. When they stopped, he stopped, and when they moved, he moved. These strangers were very dark-skinned and did not speak Greek or any language Saul knew, but they seemed friendly enough. Nevertheless, Saul watched his possessions closely and his money bag he put around his neck and down his toga, and he was very glad indeed to see the entrance way to Petra by late afternoon.

He went straight to Alexander's shop and banged on the door. Finally, the old man came and smiled when he saw Saul with a bag full of Nabatean coins.

"So you can be trusted," said Alexander.

"I should hope so", said Saul, "otherwise my God might have dealings with me as he does not like thieves!"

Saul then went straight to Miryam's abode and knocked gently at the door. It took awhile, but finally the latch slide up and she peered into the dark. "Who's there?"

"Oh just a dusty old perfume merchant," joked Saul.

"Well, come in, come in!"

---

1. This is the perfume mentioned in the story of the anointing of Jesus' feet in the Gospels. It was expensive, and also very popular, the Chanel No. 5 of its day.

And when Saul gave Miryam the vial of perfume, she blushed and said "You shouldn't have." She unstoppered it and exclaimed immediately—"It's pistic nard, now I really mean you shouldn't have. Did you have to give up your toga to get this?"

"No, only two camels (just kidding)." I wanted to get you something nice, even though, I don't even know when your birthday is."

"It's the fifth day of the month named for Augustus, next month. Are you hungry?"

"I thought you'd never ask. That piece of bread I had for breakfast gave out a while back. I'm just back from Aela, where I had to deliver some tents."

"Better watch out. That Alexander will work you into an early grave."

They continued their simple banter, while Miryam warmed up some soup and bread. Saul was exhausted but for the first time since he had come to Petra now many months ago, Petra felt something like home. If only Miryam could see her way clear to really make a home with him, but Saul was afraid to broach that subject, for fear of rejection.

CHAPTER FOURTEEN

THE SPY

THE SANHEDRIN DID NOT BELIEVE THAT SAUL HAD SUDDENLY DISAPpeared off the face of the earth. Caiaphas in particular did not believe it and wanted to extract his pound of flesh from the scoundrel. The man knew too much about the inner workings of the Sanhedrin and its secret plans for the future, and Caiaphas in his paranoia had begun to wonder if Saul of Tarsus had been a Christ-following spy within Caiaphas' network for some time. In any case, he needed to be found and tried just like the Jews he had brought to Caiaphas previously.

So it was that Caiaphas sent a team to Damascus to figure out what had become of Saul, mindful of the fact that Damascus was now Nabatean territory and his team would need to tread lightly while doing their investigating. But when the team arrived in Damascus, the trail had gone cold. After all, it had been many months since he disappeared. After much fruitless searching, Isaac, the head of the investigative team said, "The old man is near death, and we need to give him some answers before he is gathered to our ancestors.[1] Let the team go back to Jerusalem and give an interim report. I will send Joseph north to Antioch to see if Saul might be there. There are many Jews there, and it does not seem likely Saul would be unwise enough to go stay in a city even better connected with Jerusalem than Damascus, but still we must check. As for me, I will go down to Petra and sniff around and see what is to be learned. I can recognize the man

---

1. Caiaphas ceased to be high priest in about AD 37, and his probable ossuary has been found. It seems likely he died in 37–38, which is why a new high priest had to be chosen.

on sight, and if he is there, I shall find him." This plan was agreeable to the team, and so they went their separate ways.

Meanwhile, back in Petra, romance was blooming rapidly. Miryam had told Saul she was prepared to hear more about this Jesus of Nazareth, and Saul had reassured her that he had not ceased to believe there was only one God, Yahweh, but he also believed there was one Lord, Jesus Christ, the messiah of his people.[2] This seemed to calm the qualms of Miryam, and before too long, Saul was emboldened to ask Miryam if she would marry him.

A coy smile came over Miryam's face: "Are you sure you want to ask me that question?"

A queasy feeling crept into Saul's stomach, "Yes . . . and I'm holding my breath."

"I'll say yes on one condition."

"OK, anything!"

"The beard has to go. It will not only tickle, it will scratch up my face, as I have very tender skin."

Saul exhaled and said, "No problem! There is a barber in Petra. Alexander uses him regularly."

"Good. Well, you go see him this morning, I will freshen up, and you can come back and kiss your bride-to-be!"

"I'll be back shortly!" And Saul left the jewelry shop whistling one of the praise psalms he especially loved. He was not a very good whistler, but who cared. Miryam had said—YES! Little did Saul know that this close shave would help him avoid another one—later.

---

2. See 1 Cor 8:6.

CHAPTER FIFTEEN

A CLOSE SHAVE ON THE WEDDING DAY

When Isaac arrived in Petra, he came with a letter of introduction to be handed over to the Nabatean scribe who supervised visits from foreign dignitaries. After initial pleasantries, Isaac asked, "Is there a Jewish synagogue in Petra, or an area where Jews live here?"

The official scratched his chin and said, "In fact no, there is no synagogue here or I would certainly know about it, nor is there a cluster of Jewish homes in this or that part of Petra. Again, I would know if there were, especially since we have recently been at war with that treacherous Galilean Herod Antipas. So, I'm afraid I can't be of much help. Of course, I am sure there are a few resident alien Jewish business persons here, since we are a trade hub, but we don't require resident aliens to register or make themselves known, unless they create some sort of major disturbance and break the law."

"Very well," said Isaac. "I guess I will just have a thorough look around before returning to Jerusalem. Thank you for your time."

———

Jewish weddings in the first century AD did not involve a service in a synagogue, nor even necessarily the presence of a Jewish official, and the only documents normally associated with such a wedding would be the bride price and dowry documents that the parents would exchange. But if the wedding involved two adults like Saul and Miryam, and there were no parents to be found, then there would simply be an open air ceremony with friends. Alexander had requisitioned his friend the owner of the winery, Yavan, to be the toastmaster at the celebration, and Miryam had gotten several of her lady friends who were sewers to make her a wedding dress. She did not want to use her previous wedding dress, as those memories were painful. The decision was made to have the wedding in a shady place, and the only really shady place was under the gigantic fig tree near the entranceway to the market square. Of course there would be many people coming and going, but the ceremony would be short, and thereafter the wedding party and guests would retreat to the cavernous winery dining area, in the largest cave next to the market square.

Saul and Miryam were both nervous, in a positive kind of way about this day. Miryam's friends had fussed over her dress and hair and even the choice of perfume endlessly. Saul for his part kept feeling his face where his beard and moustache had once taken up residence, and for good measure he had had his wiry hair trimmed as well. He looked like a new man, with his scalp and hands and feet all anointed, and his best leather sandals, recently waxed, put on, and an all-white robe chosen, suitable for the occasion.

It was actually during the final minutes of the vows where the couple was reciting to each other the famous words from Hosea: "*So I will betroth you to Me forever; I will betroth you in righteousness and justice, in loving devotion and compassion. And I will betroth you in faithfulness, and you will know the Lord*"[1] that Saul looked up and saw a man on the perimeter of the circle of friends gazing intently at Saul and Miryam. Saul recognized the man immediately—Isaac, the right-hand man of Caiaphas, but what was he doing here? Instantly Saul's euphoria turned to fear, as it dawned on him, this man was sent to track him down, and bring him back for judgment to Jerusalem. Saul's blood ran cold, but then a providential thought popped into his head. "While I clearly recognize him, perhaps he does not recognize me."

And at that same time, Isaac was saying to himself—"Yes, those are two Jews getting married, for they recite the holy prophets in their vows, but that man does not look like Saul. He looks younger, he is clean shaven, he is not wearing the tassels, nor are the scriptures bound on his forehead, nor does he have the ringlets, the beard, the moustache, and all those things characterized Saul's appearance when he let Jerusalem for Damascus. This

---

1. Hos 2:19–20.

A CLOSE SHAVE ON THE WEDDING DAY

is surely someone else." And so it was that Isaac spent the rest of the day searching in vain for Saul in all the places he could not be found. Alexander's shop was closed on this wedding day, and there were no other merchants who really knew Saul.

As the groom and bride were processing to the winery's dining hall, Miryam took Saul's hand and discovered he was shaking. "What is wrong my love?" she asked.

Saul whispered, "I think we just had a close shave, and were saved by a close shave."

Miryam laughed, "Now you are speaking in riddles. Tell me plainly what has frightened you."

"I'm pretty certain that the man that was standing at the edge of our wedding party and watching was Isaac from Jerusalem, the high priest's lackey, and it makes sense to assume he was trying to track me down and take me back to Jerusalem to face the fury of the Sanhedrin for failing to take more Christ-followers captive in Damascus and bring them to Jerusalem for swift judgment."

"Oh dear," said Miryam, "but you think perhaps your altered appearance led Isaac to think you must be someone else?"

"Indeed, and I owe my transformed appearance and happier life to you, Miryam. Perhaps this is a good example of how God weaves all things together for good for those who love him . . . As we do!"

When they arrived at the dining hall, there were the usual toasts, "L'chaim," "to life," to the new bride, to the new groom, and the guests were all settling down to a good meal and good wine. Meanwhile, a crestfallen Isaac began his journey back to Jerusalem by way of Gaza, saying over and over again to himself "that man was surely not Saul the zealous Pharisee, once betrothed to a daughter of the finest priestly family in Jerusalem. Surely not! People don't change that much in so short a time." But Isaac had not been there on Damascus road when Saul began to change in a more drastic manner than just in his appearance. People can change; in fact, they can be born again.

Marriage

Roman Marriage Customs

Marriage was a communal affair in the ancient world, that is it involved not only the two to be married, but also their parents, and the invisible expectations of society at large. Was one marrying up or down the honor ladder? Although the love of two individuals may have been involved, the parents of the children played fundamental roles in uniting couples in marriage. Social and political rationale for growing one's status, prestige, or position governed marriage more than romantic love. Many things had to be considered such as status, age, race, and sometimes even religion.[2] A period of betrothal often preceded marriage. Roman marriages had some things in common with wedding ceremonies today such as invitations, special attire, and rings. Sometimes there was also a party thrown (*sponsalia*), and gifts exchanged—some habits never die![3] If you traveled back to a Roman wedding, some practices would also be shocking. Such as a sacrifice, omens, or the bride taking the fat of an animal and smearing it on the entryway to the groom's home.[4]

Once two persons agreed to be married, called *affectio martilias*, there had to be the consent of the bride's father (the *paterfamilia*). After the marriage ceremony, the bride came under the authority of the husband. For an official Roman marriage, they also needed to possess the right to contract a valid Roman marriage (*ius conubii*). Other than that, most marriages were private agreements among Roman families. Summer seems to have always been the best time of year to get married, Romans preferred the month of June.[5] On the special day, friends and loved ones would gather in the father of the bride's house for the ceremony. A full Roman marriage (*matrimonium iustum*) could only exist if both partners were Roman citizens. This marriage was important as it allowed children to be declared rightful heirs. There do not appear to be any official marriage "licenses."

There appears to be a minimum age for marriage—around 12 for women and 14 for men.[6] Men typically married later in life as they had to go through schooling and establish a career. Women often married younger, given the ancient mortality rates, one needed to bear multiple children as the tragic reality was that some would die—not to mention the mortality rate for mothers in childbirth. Hence, the often wide age gap between men and women in both Roman and Jewish environments. In 18 BC, Augustus passed laws on marriage as part of more extensive legislation on morality. These were designed as a remedy to the perceived problem of men's reluctance to marry. It also banned marriage with prostitutes and other women of disreputable status, such as women convicted of adultery. One legal precedent, the *Lex Iulia*

---

2. Dixon, *Roman Family*, 62–63.
3. Dixon, *Roman Family*, 64.
4. Yarbrough, "Paul, Marriage, and Divorce," 409.
5. *OCD*, 928.
6. *OCD*, 928.

de maritandis ordinibus, required marriage and remarriage for men and women between certain ages and included penalties for failing to do so.[7] Tax relief was also available for those who obeyed the law. Such legislation aimed to fulfill a practical necessity of the growing empire—supply of soldiers for the army and future administrators. The laws were aimed at the wealthier classes and freedmen. Soldiers, under the rank of centurion, were not allowed to marry, a law held for a majority of the empire.[8] Not all marriages lasted, both then and now. There was no formal certificate for divorce, nor any legal administrative requirements. By the late first century BC, both women and men could initiate a divorce in Roman culture. Although unlike modern times, the children remained with the husband since they were his property. Further, only having one husband for life was still a mark of honor known as *uniuira* that highlighted this virtue.[9]

Jewish Marriage Customs

Greco-Roman marriage was one thing, Jewish marriages another. Like any ancient person, marriage was wrapped up in the construction of honor and status. It appears to be in the interest of the father to arrange marriage contracts. The choice of a spouse was a multi-faceted decision and romantic issues do not feature prominently. The families would be tied together not only legally, but economically, hence the payment of a dowry (*mohar*) in Hebrew, from the groom's family to the bride's family.[10] Some unique aspects included the marriage payment (*ketubah*). This was a payment after the marriage contract was drawn up and was done similar to a promissory note to the bride. This appears to be an innovation that was centuries in the making but ratified in the Second Temple period. The intent behind the "promissory" note was to alleviate the financial burden on the groom as the payment was nearly a year's wages at minimum (some 200 denarii). It also worked as a deterrent against divorce, because if divorce happened, the groom would have to pay back not only the dowry but the *kettubah* as well.[11]

While divorce was not as prevalent then as it is now, it still occurred. Divorce was permissible in special circumstances. The typical reason for divorce was the breaking of one's marriage vows. But what was considered a

---

7. Galinsky, *Augustan Culture,* 130; *CAH* 10:888. See also Rawson, "Marriages, Families, Households," 93–109.
8. Dixon, *Roman Family,* 92.
9. Rawson, "Marriages, Families, Households," 97.
10. Matthews, "Family, Children," 404.
11. Instone-Brewer, "Marriage and Divorce," 916.

valid reason? Here various Jewish groups had differing opinions. Vows seemed to include sexual infidelity or failure to provide (the necessities of life such as food, clothing, shelter). Later on, certain Rabbinic schools debated the grounds and definitions of "provision" or what was the minimum instance needed for divorce. Technically, both men and women could initiate a divorce, but only a husband could write the divorce certificate.[12]

On its way out in the first century was the debate over levirate marriage and the duty of male relatives to marry widows of deceased family members (based on Deut 25:5–10). Hence, Jesus' discussion of it in Luke 20:27–40. Likewise, polygamy was ruled out of practice by the Essenes at Qumran according to their internal documents and was outlawed by the Romans, except for in Judea.[13] The primary intention of marriage was to create covenant members through procreation as the fulfillment of the creation mandate in Gen 1:28.

---

12. Instone-Brewer, "Marriage and Divorce," 917.
13. Instone-Brewer, "Marriage and Divorce," 917.

CHAPTER SIXTEEN

MARITAL BLISS

There was a small oasis down the Wadi Rum towards Ruwwafa only two hours out of Petra where there was a lovely quiet inn, and Miryam had made arrangements for the newly-weds to spend their first two nights there in the comfort and luxury of a beautiful spot. Many of her jewelry clients had stayed there and raved about the place, its food, its comfortable beds, its hot springs and cool pools. Saul and Miryam arrived there just as the August sun was setting.

After a nice, slow, sumptuous dinner, the couple retired to a suite of rooms that bordered the large pond. The sky was crystal clear and a myriad of stars could be seen through the windows adjacent to their bed. Saul and Miryam however were not paying much attention to any stars, except the ones in each other's eyes. And it was Miryam, being formerly married, who took the lead in the love-making and the couple reveled in their newfound joy and ecstasy for various hours, until they fell blissfully asleep.

They were awakened by the sound of sea gulls, who had come inland to drink from the fresh water at the oasis. Saul arose and was going to find some food for him and his bride, but to his surprise, there was a tray right outside their door with some sort of delicious hot beverage, rather like mulled wine, he did not recognize, some fruit, some flat bread and hummus, some olives, dates, and delicious sweet figs, and much more.

"Breakfast is served," announced the newly-minted husband.

Wiping the sleep from her eyes, Miryam sat up in bed, smiled and said: "They think of everything here!"

"Apparently so," smiled Saul, "apparently so."

After a thanksgiving prayer and eating in silence for a while, Saul said "We have a small matter we must sort out before going back to Petra."

"Don't tell me, let me guess. Where are we going to live, considering your cave abode is too small for us both, especially with all my things. Do not worry my love, what you don't know is, actually, there are four rooms in the back of my shop, behind the large door you can see when you enter the shop. And one of those rooms is a nice large bedroom. Problem solved."

"As the first book of Torah says, 'a man shall leave his parents, and cleave to his wife' and the implication might be, he moves in with his wife.'

"A very convenient interpretation for this occasion, my scholar. In any case, we can move you out of your man cave right away, and stop paying that rent. Life is about to get better for the both of us."

"Yes. God is good, and I am very blessed to have found a wife like you at my age."

"Yes you are," Miryam joked, "and don't you ever forget it, or I will remind you."

After their brief stay at the oasis, the couple returned to Petra, moved Saul's few belongings to Miryam's house which had her shop in the front of it, and life went on without anything causing them any troubles for many months. They worked hard, as a couple it was easier to make new friends who were married, and Saul and Miryam found that their combined earnings allowed them to put away a bit of money each week, in preparation for having a family, which they talked about quite regularly. As for Saul, the one thing niggling at him was that he had done nothing yet to fulfill his calling, other than talk to his new wife about it, but he trusted God would show him when the time and opportunity was right and ripe. He had now been gone from Damascus for a year and a half, and one part of him had no desire to ever leave Petra. All the creature comforts, all the blessings of family, food, friends, meaningful work he already had in abundance in Petra. But there was one thing he had always wanted to do—take a pilgrimage to Mt. Sinai, where Moses received the ten commandments. He would broach the subject with Miryam at an opportune time, he told himself. Maybe tomorrow would be a good time, he thought.

CHAPTER SEVENTEEN

PLANNING THE JOURNEY TO JEBEL MUSA

The so-called mountain of Moses, also known as Mt. Sinai, or even Mt. Horeb, had been a site for Jewish pilgrimage centuries before Saul had ever dreamed of going there. On this morning while drinking some goat's milk and eating some fruit, he said to Miryam, who was sitting cross-legged across from him on the floor of their place, "My love, I have a longing to make one more trip before we get back to our daily routine."

"And before we have that big talk you keep promising we'll have about having children."

"Yes, and before that talk as well. I would like to do a pilgrimage to the mountain of Moses. I realize it's quite the journey, but we are both young and fit enough to make such a journey, and like Moses, I would like to go and have a talk with our God on that holy mountain about what the future augurs for us. I have a calling on my life, but it is not clear how I should fulfill it, as you already know."

"I'm not surprised to hear this request, but I'm betting you didn't know that Nabateans have been making that same pilgrimage to that holy mountain for a long time."[1] Did you know there are inscriptions in the Nabatean language at Mt. Sinai from two centuries or more ago?"

---

1. Josephus seems reasonably certain that Mt. Sinai is in the Sinai peninsula, as he says it's *between* Egypt and Arabia proper, in Arabia Petraea. See *Ant.* 2.7.1; 3.5.1.

"I did not know that, but it does not surprise me, since the Nabateans have been prominent Bedouins, traders in the region for many centuries, and they are a highly religious people as well."[2]

"And you are in luck. Wafi, my friend whom I do jewelry business with from time to time, was in the past a guide to Sinai and back. I'm sure we could pay him to guide us."

"Excellent. I like the way you think. Is there a local map we could look at?"

"Yes, Wafi has the maps, but I think I borrowed one from him, and have not returned it yet. Let me look in my desk for a minute. Ah . . . here it is."

"So basically, we must travel to Aela, sail south down the gulf to Ohahab, and then hike overland to the mountain range that includes Mt. Sinai." This will take four to five days at least, each way. Those mountains are higher than any here in Arabia proper. Sinai is actually the second tallest peak in that range, but plenty high enough to be close to God. We will need to pack lots of foodstuffs, so I'll get busy with that task, and run down to Wafi's place, and see what it will take to get him to guide us."

"And I'll run to Alexander's and tell him, never fear, I'm coming back, but we have to make a pilgrimage to a holy mountain first. He will groan, but nonetheless understand. Anyway, business is a bit slow these days. So the trip shouldn't trouble him much."

"The question is," said Miryam, "what are we expecting to see or hear when we get there?"

"Perhaps that whisper, that still small voice, that Elijah spoke of," said Saul, "and did you know that the Elijah story is the last reference to the Holy Mountain in all our sacred texts?"

---

2. Wikipedia provides good general information: "The traditional Mount Sinai, located in the Sinai Peninsula, is actually the name of a collection of peaks, sometimes referred to as the Holy Mountain peaks which consist of Jebel Musa, Mount Catherine and Ras Sufsafeh. Etheria (circa fourth century AD) wrote, 'The whole mountain group looks as if it were a single peak, but, as you enter the group, [you see that] there are more than one.' The highest mountain peak is Mount Catherine, rising 2,610 metres (8,550 feet) above the sea and its sister peak, Jebel Musa (2,285 m [7,497 ft]), is not much further behind in height, but is more conspicuous because of the open plain called *er Rachah* ('the wide'). Mount Catherine and Jebel Musa are both much higher than any mountains in the Sinaitic desert, or in all of Midian. The highest tops in the Tih desert to the north are not much over 1,200 m (4,000 ft). Those in Midian, East of Elath, rise only to 1,300 m (4,200 ft). Even Jebel Serbal, 30 km (20 mi) west of Sinai, is at its highest only 2,050 m (6,730 ft) above the sea" (https://en.wikipedia.org/wiki/Biblical_Mount_Sinai).

Miryam smiled: "Leave it to my scholar to add an educational note, when I was thinking more romantically about that mountain." They both laughed, and you could tell they were excited about the pilgrimage and its revelations, but they had not anticipated how much it would reveal to them about themselves.

CHAPTER EIGHTEEN

WAFI IN THE LEAD

Wafi was irrepressible. Not a Nabatean but rather an Ethiopian, he had been making journeys all his life across the deserts of Sinai below Egypt. Standing all of five feet tall and sharing the deep black skin of his fellow Ethiopians, Wafi sought to enhance his stature by wearing a big turban on his head, which doubled as a scarf he could pull across his face when the wind and the sand began blowing in all directions. Wafi's three camels were named for the patriarchs—Abraham, Isaac, and Jacob and like the patriarchs, they were used to long pilgrimages in the general direction of some part of Egypt. Nothing would deter them from pressing forward to their goal.

As they mounted up Wafi said to the newlyweds, "these camels have a lot of miles on them, so we must be kind to them. We will not require them to trot very much but rather to take long walking strides, and at that pace, we should arrive at Mt. Sinai, on the fourth day of our pilgrimage, God willing and no bad weather occurs. Here is where I tell you that I too am a Jew, an Ethiopian Jew, and we believe that we have the ark of the covenant itself in a safe place in Ethiopia, brought to us by no less than the descendants of the Queen of Sheba. You see when the Babylonians came to conquer Jerusalem, the priests could not allow them to take the ark into Babylon and so it was packed off to be cared for by Jews, perhaps first at Sinai, and then much later, when Sinai was in peril from bandits and thieves, it was taken to Axum in Ethiopia where it resides today."[1]

---

1. The Ethiopian Orthodox legends about this are traced back to the early Middle Ages. See https://en.wikipedia.org/wiki/Ark_of_the_Covenant.

"That's an interesting legend," said Saul, "and perhaps there is some truth in it after all. For sure, the ark is not in Jerusalem now, and has not been for centuries. In fact, some of us have issues with Herod's temple as well, but that's a story for another day. Wafi, tell us how you came to live in Petra."

"Gladly, but you two must tell me how you came to be married."

"Fair enough, but you first," said Saul.

"I am the son of traders who roamed Ethiopia, Egypt, the Sinai peninsula, and the Nabatean land. We also occasionally went up to Jerusalem for the festivals.[2] Our stock and trade was spices, easy to transport, never likely to spoil, and always in demand everywhere in the region—spices for beverages, spices for food, incense for ceremonies, for burial rituals, and yes also perfumes as well especially for the royals and the ladies in general. As far as I can tell, my family going back four generations has been doing this. We observe Torah a bit differently than the Jews in Judea and Galilee, but basically it is the same religion about the one God and the one collection of sacred texts. I have three brothers and sisters, all in the same trade, but they live in Ethiopia and Egypt, I am, so to speak, their foreign agent, gathering the spices in Petra as they have come up the spice road from the South. And now it is your turn to tell your tale, but look—we have already arrived at the first oasis. Let's first let the camels drink, and then slake our own thirst."

The goal of the first day of the journey was to reach Aela, perhaps shortly after dark. Wafi had made arrangements for a place to stay, and the following morning bright and early, they would all be on a large felucca, camels and all sailing down the gulf for more than a full day. The journey then becomes quite arduous over mountains and through ravines until one finally arrives at Mt. Sinai, the mountain of God. They only paused briefly at the oasis, and carried on straight to Aela, arriving as anticipated just at dusk.

Sitting around an open fire near the sea, Wafi finally asked: "Will you please tell me your story? How did you two meet and come together?"

Looking at Miryam, Saul said, "Shall I start?" and she nodded.

"My story could take a long time to tell, but I will give a brief synopsis. I was born in Tarsus in Cilicia, to parents who were devout Jews, indeed my father was a Pharisee and also a Roman citizen, which is how I became both of these things, following in his footsteps. I learned as well the family trade of making tents out of *cilicium* as well as making other leather products.

---

2. On which compare Acts 8:26–40.

I was bright, and my father wanted the best Pharisaic education for me, which meant that before I had come of age we had all moved to Jerusalem, and I had become the understudy of Gamaliel, one of the great Pharisaic teachers, and I became one of his more challenging students for reasons that will become obvious in a few minutes.

"I was one of those persons who thought that zeal for the Law included protecting God's people from false teachings and practices, even if it meant treating some fellow Jews as beyond the pale, indeed as blasphemers deserving the forty lashes, or even stoning. You could call this the excessive zeal of youth, or even a zeal 'not according to knowledge'. In any case, it led to me being the 'hit' man for the Sanhedrin in regards to this new sect of the followers of Jesus of Nazareth, who even in spite of his being crucified, considered him the Jewish messiah, and more. Now, this seemed absurd to me, and so I was happy to be designated to deal with this problem. But then something unexpected, indeed drastic happened to me.

"I was traveling with companions to extradite various Christ-followers living in Damascus and bring them back for trial before the Sanhedrin, when suddenly I was flattened on the road just outside of Damascus by a heavenly being whom I saw in a vision."

"You mean an angel, no doubt?" interjected Wafi.

"No, actually I mean the risen and exalted Jesus himself, who asked me why I was persecuting him, an odd question from a heavenly being, until it dawned on me he meant his followers of course. Right then he began to reveal himself to me, and commission me to do the opposite of what I had been doing—instead of snuffing out this new messianic movement, I was to lead the way in sharing the good news about Jesus with non-Jews."

"Extraordinary," said Wafi. "You are sure you weren't drunk or sun-struck?"

"Neither, but I was blinded by the experience and had to be led by the hand into Damascus, where through the good help of a Jewish Christ-follower named Ananias, I received some of my sight back, was baptized, and became a Christ-follower myself. The old Saul was left behind in Damascus. But what was the new Saul to do? And where could he go? Clearly, not back to Jerusalem where he might himself be tried by the Sanhedrin, and would hardly be likely to receive a warm welcome from the Christ-followers of Judea whom he had persecuted, even to the point of the death of one them named Stephanos."

"Well, I was already in newly claimed Nabatean territory in Damascus, so the thought occurred to me to come to Petra and make a new start where the Sanhedrin's spies would be unlikely to find me. And so I did. I will let Miryam continue the story at this point."

"One day, this man with a scruffy beard and moustache came into my jewelry shop in Petra. As you already know Wafi, I had lost my husband over a year ago and had just finished my period of mourning for him. I was certainly not looking for a new husband at the time, not least because I had my own resources and was pretty much self-sufficient by the help of our gracious God. But there was something about this man Saul I found intriguing, and even charming—except of course for the scruffy facial hair, which mercifully he has shaved off at my request, and may it ever be so. Gradually, over some weeks and months I reckon we fell in love and yet I was surprised how soon he asked me if I would marry him, and I surprised myself by saying yes . . . and I'm glad I did."

Wafi smiled and said, "You seem like a well-matched couple, and I wish you every blessing, including the blessing of children if it be God's will."

"We are so newly-wed, that we haven't even had that conversation yet!" laughed Miryam, "but I'm sure we shall before long."

With that, the three of them turned in for the night.

CHAPTER NINETEEN

SAILING SOUTH

Dawn came early, signaled by the cock crowing, and the trio were up quickly, leading their camels to the waiting felucca. The captain of the boat named Jonah, was also a fellow Jew and a good friend of Wafi's. They cast off immediately once all were on board with their goods and animals, and set sail due South. There was a nice breeze as the sun rose in the sky, and the sheer beauty of the scene was impressive.

The sailing was enjoyable, even peaceful. There were no storms, no pirates or trouble-makers to bother them, and the only boats they saw were large boats heading to Aela to off-load their cargo. In fact, the whole day was spent just coasting along before docking on the Sinai peninsula.

"This is the easy and enjoyable part of our journey," said Wafi, "but soon the camels will be grunting as we work our way through the mountainous region leading to Mt. Sinai. Our journey becomes much slower and deliberate once we dock."

Wafi had not said anything in reaction to Saul's personal account, and he found it most puzzling, prompting a thousand questions, but he had held his tongue, waiting for an opportune minute to ask a few pertinent things. Like most ancients, Wafi believed that people's personalities and life directions are set from birth, determined by gender, generation, and even geography, determined by whether one was male or female, determined by whose son or daughter one was, determined by where one was born. This whole way of thinking, to Wafi's mind, was reflected by the early part of Saul's story, and the fact that he called himself Saul of Tarsus. Wafi like other Jews knew the proverbs like "can a leopard change its spots?" to which the answer was an emphatic no. The concept of real transformation in mid or late life was a new idea to Wafi, and it was a puzzle to him. Had Saul really had a vision of a heavenly Jesus that totally changed the direction of his life? He admitted that visions were possible, but was it possible that the one and only God had a son, named Jesus, whom he exalted to his right hand after crucifixion and resurrection? Wafi knew of no scriptures that predicted a crucified and risen messiah, much less that the messiah would also be a divine Son of God. So there was indeed much to ponder, and he felt he must choose his questions carefully, as he liked his friend Miryam and did not want to offend those who were paying him.

After they got settled in tents near the dock, and darkness had descended on the travelers, they gathered for a light meal of bread, wine, fruit, and nuts, and it was near the end of the meal that Wafi quietly asked, "Saul, I find your testimony quite interesting. My question is—'Are you sure it was Jesus and not some guardian angel that was complaining about your persecutions of fellow Jews, say the angel Michael?'"

"Yes, quite sure. He identified himself clearly, and it was a total shock to me. I would never have anticipated such a revelation, or have believed it myself if it hadn't been so clear and convincing. Remember, I despised Jesus and his followers before this revelation, thought they were ruining our good faith in the one God."

"OK," said Wafi. "There is much about our God that is a mystery, so I must ponder this some more. Meanwhile, we should turn in early, as tomorrow is going to be arduous and long."

Miryam and Saul agreed, and they snuffed out their little campfire, and turned in for the night. But as Saul and Miryam were heading for their tent, Saul looked up and recited one of his favorite psalms: "when I consider the works of thy hands, the sun, the moon, the stars—What is a human being that you should be mindful of him, or the son of man that thou should care? And yet you have made him but a little lower than the angels."

"The sky is so full of stars tonight," said Miryam. "And yet God does care about each one of us, or he would not have led you to the door of a lonely and sad jewelry saleswoman like me."

"Nor would he have led a man without a people or a family, to a person as special as you, Miryam, if he had abandoned me."

"Amen and amen," they both said together.

CHAPTER TWENTY

A LONG DAY'S JOURNEY INTO NIGHT

The journey through the mountain range to Mt. Sinai was not for the faint of heart, out of shape, those with a fear of heights, or lacking a sense of adventure, or those not really determined to make the trip. Even the camels complained about this part of the journey and rightly so. The terrain was rugged at best, the paths up the mountain paths often serpentine, and one had to impress oneself up against the rock wall when a caravan was coming down the mountain going in the opposite direction. Not a lot of talking transpired, so hard were the three travelers concentrating on looking straight ahead and holding on the saddle on their camels. While Wafi was used to this journey, Saul and Miryam were not and their eyes drank in the unfamiliar scenery at every turn. They would not soon forget this trek.

At one point Saul recited to himself another of his favorites psalms—"Even though I walk through the valley of the shadow of deep darkness, I shall fear no evil, for You are with me. Your rod and staff they comfort me. . . ." Sometimes they would turn a corner and see a plateau in the mountains.

Sometimes there seemed no end in sight to the mountains. Would they ever get to Mt. Sinai, and would their thighs ever stop aching from riding day after a long day on uncomfortable camels? They became weary and saddlesore, which produced two silent travelers, while Wafi out front seemed to be enjoying the journey.

Yet they kept traveling on, drinking a bit of wine, eating a bit of bread, and carrying on. Even though it was not winter, the mountainous desert was cold at night, and so each night Wafi built a fire. One of those nights he said to his weary friends, "So I have a tale to tell you, a Jewish legend of sorts. The story goes that when Hagar was first cast out from her Abrahamic family, with her child Ishmael, she headed south in the direction of Egypt, being from Egypt in the first place, and went on pilgrimage all the way to Mt. Sinai to find God's answer about her future. She was reassured that what God had first told Abraham was true—'And as for Ishmael, I have heard you: I will surely bless him; I will make him fruitful and will greatly increase his numbers. He will be the father of twelve rulers, and I will make him into a great nation.' Now some Bedouins I know who live in the Sinai peninsula believe they are the descendants of Ishmael, and that the land should be rightfully theirs. What do you think of this tale?"

Saul spoke up and said, "I suppose it's possible. That story in the first book of Torah is very allusive and not full of details. In the middle of that book, we are told that Isaac and Ishmael together buried their father Abraham in the cave of Machpelah.[1] There must have been some reconciliation or peace between Isaac and Ishmael at some point."

Wafi smiled and said: "Well, enough with campfire tales. We must get some rest. Tomorrow we reach the holy mountain."

---

1. Gen 25:9. Cf. Gen 16 for the earlier part of the story. Gen 25:17 says he lived to age 137.

CHAPTER TWENTY-ONE

THE MOUNTAIN OF MOSES

When first seen from afar, Jebel Musa seems to be several mountains in one, which is in fact correct. And Mt. Sinai is not the highest peak in that range.

The view from above, as our travelers would soon learn was spectacular, especially at sunset, and sunset was exactly when the travelers finally reached the peak of the mountain of Moses and took in the view. The climb to the top had obviously been undertaken by many pilgrims because part of the way up there were actually carefully placed stone stairs and an archway, where according to tradition Moses saw the back of God's form. Saul had always wondered about that story, since God was spirit, and did not have a physical form. But then perhaps God could manifest himself in any way he pleased, being almighty.

The trio sat at the top watching the sun go down, and Wafi stressed, "We must descend soon as the descent becomes treacherous in the dark what with the winds. So say your prayers if you wish, and then we must begin going down." Saul went over to a cliff edge, wrapped his mantle around his head, while Miryam watched from a few feet away with Wafi.

"What does the still small voice that spoke to Elijah and Moses say to me?" asked Saul. "How shall I fulfill my commission?" Then Saul listened intently and in his mind he heard an answer—"Go back. Go back, and share the Good News in Petra, and some will believe. But there will be a cost, and heartache too." Sobered by what he believed he had been told, he took Miryam's hand, and said, "Yes, it is time to go down, though it is starkly beautiful up here. One can imagine Moses and Elijah talking with God here." And so they went down to the base camp, where they had pitched their tents in the afternoon, and reflected on a day they would never forget. Much later Saul would write in one of his earliest letters . . .

"Tell me, you who want to be under the law, are you not aware of what the law says? For it is written that Abraham had two sons, one by the slave woman and the other by the free woman. His son by the slave woman was born according to the flesh, but his son by the free woman was born as the result of a divine promise. These things are being taken figuratively: The women represent two covenants. One covenant is from Mount Sinai and bears children who are to be slaves: This is Hagar. Now Hagar stands for Mount Sinai in Arabia and corresponds to the present city of Jerusalem, because she is in slavery with her children. But the Jerusalem that is above is free, and she is our mother. For it is written:

'Be glad, barren woman,
you who never bore a child;
shout for joy and cry aloud,
you who were never in labor;
because more are the children of the desolate woman
than of her who has a husband.'

Now you, brothers and sisters, like Isaac, are children of promise. At that time the son born according to the flesh persecuted the son born by the power of the Spirit. It is the same now. But what does Scripture say? 'Get rid of the slave woman and her son, for the slave woman's son will never share in the inheritance with the free woman's son.' Therefore, brothers and sisters, we are not children of the slave woman, but of the free woman."

CHAPTER TWENTY-TWO

THE RETURN TO THE SEA

Much was on Saul's mind as they traveled back to the sea. For one thing, it had been close to two years since he left Damascus. He assumed that things had quieted down, since no one had come and taken him away to Jerusalem for trial, and the one emissary who did come to Petra fortunately did not recognize him. And that was some eight months prior to this journey. Saul was feeling relatively secure that his zealous past was not catching up with him. But what of his foretold future? What was he to do about that, especially now that he and Miryam were happily married. Just then Miryam interrupted Saul's reverie.

"OK, husband, it's time to have the talk about babies."

"Right here, right now while riding along behind Wafi."

"Yes, right here, right now."

"OK, but I have a question first. Why were there no children with your first husband?"

"I figured you'd ask, sooner or later. We tried, unsuccessfully to have children, but God did not bless us with any, and then, as you know, my husband died."

"Well, when we get back to 'Rock City' we can begin to try to have a family, but I will let you decide when the opportune time will be."

"Very wise, husband. Very wise. We will talk more of this soon."

When they arrived at the sea, and even though this was not the body of water that his ancestors crossed with Moses "on dry ground," Saul nonetheless began thinking about the connections between that story and his own "sea crossing" so to speak, into a new life in another land. He wondered about the analogies between that Exodus, and that of Christ-followers.[1] Saul did not believe that the lessons of the past should or could be ignored, as if irrelevant to his present situation. He knew that apostasy from the faith was possible for believers, including for himself, and he knew that the Lord was watching him, wanting him to get on with sharing his newfound faith in the crucified and risen One. But how to do it? And with whom? And where? Petra now seemed to Saul, with the benefit of knowing the place for a while, as perhaps less open than some places in the Greco-Roman part of the empire to a proclamation about Jesus. Yet he must try.

"Husband, you seem lost in thought. May I ask what's on your heart?"

"Yes, Miryam, I am conscious that I have not yet done what the heavenly vision commissioned me to do, and so I keep pondering when and how and whereto share the Good News about a crucified and risen Savior. Yet, at the same time, I do not wish to upset our newfound domestic tranquility and love for each other. You must pray for me to see the doors God is opening, and be brave enough to walk through them. I must not allow a comfortable present to get in the way of going forward on faith into the future as God's servant and emissary."

"Yes, as you say, you must obey God, and sometimes that means not relying on one's natural instincts and preferences. Still, I believe God has brought us together into this marriage for times such as these. Let us make the most of this blessing."

"Indeed, I agree wholeheartedly."

The crossing of the sea over to Aela was uneventful, as the water was very calm on this day. Wafi himself had been lost in thought, wondering what to make of Saul and his "commission." What he had decided for the time being is to say nothing to anyone about it, as he did not want to imperil his few Jewish friends in Petra by reporting Saul to the authorities. He had to hope Saul would not make a scene, and thereby imperil all of the small cadre of Jews in Petra, including himself and his own family.

---

1. In fact, he ponders these analogies at length in 1 Cor 10.

CHAPTER TWENTY-THREE

DOMESTIC FERTILITY OR FUTILITY?

When Saul and Miryam got home to Petra, they began in earnest to try and and have a family. Miryam had some convictions about certain times of the month being more propitious than others, and of course they would avoid the period of uncleanness in deference to what Jewish Law says about that period of blood flow. Some months went by, until one day over breakfast and before Saul went off to Alexander's shop, Miryam announced proudly, "I believe I am now with child. My cycle is very regular, and I have now missed two periods of blood flow in a row."

Saul's eyes got big, and a huge smile broke across his face: "Really? You really think a child may be on the way?"

"I do indeed, and we now need to pray to God for the safety of the child throughout the pregnancy. I'm glad we are through with traveling for a while, and I will be sticking close to home, and just working quietly in the shop for the next months until the baby comes. Wafi's wife is in fact a midwife, so we will call upon her services when the time comes."

For once in his life, the loquacious man from Tarsus was speechless. "I am to be a father," mumbled Saul to himself. "God is good!" And so the couple had a brief prayer, holding hands, for divine supervision of the coming months of the pregnancy.

Not surprisingly, when Saul got to Alexander's shop he was, and seemed to be rather distracted and Alexander noticed. "Is there something troubling you, Saul?"

DOMESTIC FERTILITY OR FUTILITY?

"To the contrary, my friend. I am marveling at God's goodness. It seems my Miryam is with child."

"Congratulations! That's wonderful news. Selfishly, I am glad to hear this as I assume it means you'll not be leaving Petra anytime soon, and I can count on your good work into the future. You know my shop has really done well since I hired you, and I'd like to keep going in that direction. To that end, I think I shall give you a bit of a raise, as you need now to be saving for the new member of your family."

"Alexander, that is very kind, and much needed and appreciated. I shall continue to work hard, and try and do good quality work as well."

"I know you will. Again congratulations. This is good news." But immediately a cloud came over Saul's joy, for a little voice inside his head said, "Yes, this is good news, but not the Good News God has commissioned you to share with others." And this thought would continue to trouble Saul in the weeks to come. The longer the pregnancy went, the more anxious Saul became about what he was to do about his commission and when to do it, and with whom. And a further troubling thought was that he had been afraid to ask Miryam what she thought, after some months of pondering, about this Jesus whom Saul now believed was the risen Lord. What good was being a herald if you couldn't convince your own wife to embrace the message? He resolved to talk with her some more about the Good News, and see how things developed. He needed to go back and unroll his scrolls of Isaiah, and contemplate some more what that prophet said about the Good News.

The work in the tent-making and leather-working shop was often demanding not least because while average citizens might be prepared to wait a while for what they needed, since the matter was not urgent (who needs a new wineskin immediately, or even new sandals?), but when an emissary from the king, or some other official came needing something urgently— like five new tents by Friday, then one found oneself working night and day during that week to get the job done on time. The work could be tedious, tiring, time-consuming, and simply exhausting, especially the stitching part of the job. During such a week, Saul regularly came home well after dark, too tired to even eat much, and needing to go right to bed, since he had to be up at dawn and off to work again. Miryam entirely understood this temporary "emergency work schedule" but it did frustrate her at times, wanting to spend more time with Saul as the pregnancy developed.

Finally, during a lull in such urgent work, Saul and Miryam had a day to catch up on things, and Saul finally mustered up his courage and asked, "Now that you've had some time to mull over my story about the Good News about Jesus of Nazareth, tell me what you are thinking about it."

"Saul, I love you, and I respect your intellect and convictions, and I too was taught from an early age to hope for and look for the Jewish messiah. That part is not a problem. I just have difficulty believing God would allow his special anointed one to be crucified, and then raised from the dead. Why? Why was that necessary?"

Fresh from contemplating more of Isaiah, Saul said, "There is a good reason—namely our sins and especially our deliberate sins which could not be atoned for under Mosaic provisions. You will remember there is no atonement for so-called sins with a 'high hand.' None in the Torah. And yet even God's people, even God's leaders like David and Solomon as well as ordinary folk have committed many such sins. While he does not mention crucifixion per se, Isaiah I think does speak to this matter. Let me grab my scroll and read to you what I was contemplating last night before we blew out the lamps.

> 'See, my servant will act wisely;
>> he will be raised and lifted up and highly exalted.
> Just as there were many who were appalled at him—
>> his appearance was so disfigured beyond that of any human being
>> and his form marred beyond human likeness—
> so he will sprinkle many nations,
>> and kings will shut their mouths because of him.
> For what they were not told, they will see,
>> and what they have not heard, they will understand.
> Who has believed our message
>> and to whom has the arm of the Lord been revealed?
> He grew up before him like a tender shoot,
>> and like a root out of dry ground.
> He had no beauty or majesty to attract us to him,
>> nothing in his appearance that we should desire him.
> He was despised and rejected by mankind,
>> a man of suffering, and familiar with pain.
> Like one from whom people hide their faces
>> he was despised, and we held him in low esteem.
> Surely he took up our pain

and bore our suffering,
yet we considered him punished by God,
> stricken by him, and afflicted.
But he was pierced for our transgressions,
> he was crushed for our iniquities;
the punishment that brought us peace was on him,
> and by his wounds we are healed.
We all, like sheep, have gone astray,
> each of us has turned to our own way;
and the Lord has laid on him
> the iniquity of us all.
He was oppressed and afflicted,
> yet he did not open his mouth;
he was led like a lamb to the slaughter,
> and as a sheep before its shearers is silent,
> so he did not open his mouth.
By oppression and judgment he was taken away.
> Yet who of his generation protested?
For he was cut off from the land of the living;
> for the transgression of my people he was punished.
He was assigned a grave with the wicked,
> and with the rich in his death,
though he had done no violence,
> nor was any deceit in his mouth.
Yet it was the Lord's will to crush him and cause him to suffer,
> and though the Lord makes[j] his life an offering for sin,
he will see his offspring and prolong his days,
> and the will of the Lord will prosper in his hand.
After he has suffered,
> he will see the light of life and be satisfied;
by his knowledge my righteous servant will justify many,
> and he will bear their iniquities.
Therefore I will give him a portion among the great,
> and he will divide the spoils with the strong,
because he poured out his life unto death,
> and was numbered with the transgressors.
For he bore the sin of many,
> and made intercession for the transgressors.'"

Miryam pondered this for a while, and then said, "Isn't 'my servant' a term for the nation of Israel, rather than a particular individual?"

"Excellent question! I used to think that as well since it's clear from earlier in these poetic prophecies that Israel is called 'my servant', but when one gets to this juncture in Isaiah, it seems clear that he is referring to a particular person offering himself as an atonement for sin. And notice it is the Almighty's will both that he suffer and die, and then beyond death be vindicated and exalted, and be given 'a portion with the great'. This, it seems to me, clearly foreshadows or even predicts the end of Jesus' earthly ministry and life."

After a pause, Miryam said, "Yes, I can see that. I had never thought of that part of Isaiah that way before, but now that suffering servant passage makes better sense. Our sins had to be dealt with, even especially our intentional and willful violations of known laws. Only the servant could wipe clean that slate andatone for such heinous transgressions.[1] So husband, I will contemplate this, and see if I too can embrace this Good News, and join you in that belief. Give me some time to pray about this."

"Of course," said a relieved Saul. "I long for us to be one in the Spirit and in the Lord, as well as in the Father and the Holy Scriptures which we already embrace together."

Ancient Families

The world is, and always has been, made up of people walking this planet. These people organize into social groups, often referred to as a family. These families are made up of men, women, children, husbands, and wives. But how do ancient families compare? What was similar and different from the modern concept of the family and the expectations for those within? Key terms are in order. Most ancient persons were concerned not with the *familia* but with the *Domus* or house. Household management (*oikonomia*) was was central to ancient thinking about families and society. The household unit was considered the beating heart of many ancient societies. Since all societies are made-up of social units, the smallest social unit was the individual home (*oikos* in Greek, *Domus* in Latin). One might think of these as nesting dolls, houses make up cities, cities make up empires. Thus, control of one's house, when seen as a part

---

1. Notice in Acts 13, Paul is portrayed as making precisely this point—"Therefore, my friends, I want you to know that through Jesus the forgiveness of sins is proclaimed to you. Through him everyone who believes is set free from every sin, a justification you were not able to obtain under the law of Moses."

DOMESTIC FERTILITY OR FUTILITY?

of a much larger whole, was very important. Divisions at home or mismanaged houses could lead to mismanaged cities, and mismanaged empires. One can quickly see the logic at work. The term family (*familia*) thus is complicated as it more often refers to things or property. Sadly, it often refers to "family" of slaves connected to a house.[2]

Any ancient definition of family (*oikos, domus, familia*) is complicated by the fact that the ancient world was a slave society and each of these terms included that element in its definition of house or family (see slavery closer look). These terms in the ancient world are much more expansive than the modern concept of "nuclear family." One often neglected aspect in this discussion is what ancient Romans honored in terms of familial relationships. We get a clue as to what they valued by looking at the inscriptions on tombstones:

> In a landmark analysis of all the epitaphs of Rome and most of the western empire, in 1984 Saller and Shaw revealed that overwhelmingly the relationships commemorated were those of the close biological family, what we call the 'nuclear family'. The bond most often recorded in the epitaphs is that of spouses and of parents and children. This does not tell the whole story of household structure, or other personal relationships. . .but it tells a story of what relationships commemorators wished to record and leave for posterity. These were surely their closest affective relationships.[3]

Much of our knowledge of ancient Roman families comes from large, well-to-do members of society. It is much harder to know, apart from material culture (house size, rooms, utensils, etc.), how smaller households functioned. High status families would typically include not only the husband, wife, children, and slaves, but could also include other relatives, sometimes visitors, and even workers. The small apartment-style houses of the lower classes would not have been large enough to accommodate much more than a biological family and possibly one or two slaves.

Men

One of the highest social classes in the ancient world was that of the male, free born, Roman citizen. Roman men had immense power in all social realms. The Roman *familia* was lead by the oldest male (*paterfamilias*). Fathers exercised immense power over the lives of their families, which would include their spouse, children, grandchildren, and slaves. As a father, their power granted

---

2. Dixon, *Roman Family*, 2.
3. Rawson, "Marriages, Families, Households," 101.

legal marriages and even controlled economic functions of their family. In fact, a son only left the power of his father, on the father's death. This idea has been challenged as it only appears mostly in legal documents and occurs mainly in large estate contexts. Interestingly it rarely used to actually describe fathers.[4] Despite the debate, the history of marriage and family is a story of the "very slow erosion of powers of the *paterfamilias*, both as father and husband."[5]

Women

One challenge with our ancient sources on this topic is that almost all of them are written by men so what we see represented and discussed are male views on the topic. Relatively little remains by way of literary evidence from female writers. We know that women could read and write, although not the same percentage as men. Their literacy rates were tied to various tasks needed to run an ancient household or conduct affairs in business (receipts, purchase orders, and the writing of requests). Sadly, women were viewed as the biological and intellectual inferiors of men. Medical textbooks and philosophical treatises bear out these sad realities.[6]

Women can and did earn property (*tutela*) and by the late republic and empire, the form of marriage preferred (called *sine manu*) retained her property to stay with her family of origin.[7] Dowry was a different matter altogether, which did transfer from the father of the bride to the husband. This was usually a sum of money to take care of the daughter/wife for the duration of the marriage. Wealthy women had more power and honor in ancient Rome than most and could have both formal and informal roles in civic life. Lower-class women worked outside the home.

One of the primary roles, across the millennia, for women was bearing legitimate children for her husband. Heirs were needed for the inheritance laws of the ancient world. The trajectory of most women's lives was to make the transition up the social categories from daughter and sister to being wife and mother. These roles were always under the guardianship of a male relation (father or husband). The role of the mother varied depending on social status. Often children were kept and raised by slaves if the family could afford it. The important role of a *pedagogue* or instructor/teacher was that of moral guide aimed with raising the child.

---

4. Cohick, "Women, Children, and Families," 180.
5. Dixon, *Roman Family*, 77.
6. *OCD*, 1623.
7. Neils, "Women in Rome," 7:250–51.

Children

Many factors shape the radical difference between ancient and modern conceptions of childhood. In the modern west, there is a romanticization of childhood and a keen sense of developing stages with an eye to intense care and nurturing of children. The Roman world, and other ancient cultures, looked at childhood very differently. First, the high infant mortality rate left little to be romanticized. Recent research has put the mortality rate at nearly 35 percent of newborn babies within the first month and a shocking 50 percent would die by the age of ten.[8] The goal was that the child survived; thriving was a whole other matter. Ancient moralists and philosophers have somewhat of a detachment to small children that may be rooted in this harsh reality. Second, caregivers provided a buffer between parent and child. A slave or wet-nurse would be the primary caregiver in these situations. They cared deeply for the children, as probably their parents did as well. We should be cautious not to read in a bias to ancient texts. To give a modern example, two working parents care just as much for their children even though they use a nanny or daycare services, as a stay at home parent. A third reason, is that from a philosophical point of view children were guided by their passions and not by virtue—indeed this was the main aim of the pedagogue or teacher to instill wisdom and virtue to control the passions. Thus there is not much to observe or learn from a child, it is simply a stage on the journey of life and the quicker one gains virtue the better. This makes Jesus' and the early Christians' valuing of children (to become like a child to enter the kingdom) all the more radical in this ancient context.

Children who did overcome the immense barriers to thriving in life (war, disease, famine) would be trained at home until schooling (if the family could afford it). There were no public school systems. Most sons would go on to learn the trade of their father, and possibly their father's father. Apprenticing was the primary form of education in the ancient world. Daughters were trained at home, usually by the mother, in domestic skills. The ancient home was also a business of sorts, so in addition to the more traditional childhood expectations, children would also become adept at many aspects of business until the time they would be married off and begin the same process themselves.

---

8. Laes, *Children in the Roman Empire*, 26.

CHAPTER TWENTY-FOUR

A DAY OF DREAD

Some six months into her pregnancy, Miryam began to bleed, which was not a good sign. She consulted Wafi's wife, and was given a serum laced with honey, which seemed to stop the flow ... for a few days. But then it happened again and Miryam began to think she needed to stop normal activities and confine herself to the house, with minimal walking around. She told Saul about this, but he understood little of these matters, and simply devoted more time to praying for Miryam and the baby. But clearly, he was very worried. Saul knew of cases where women miscarried, and even worse cases where women died in giving birth to a child. He did not want either of those things to happen to his Miryam. What Miryam had not told Saul, is that she had been pregnant once before, when married to her first husband, and had a miscarriage early in the pregnancy, well before the six month. That had been many years ago, and she did not think she needed to bring it up when she and Saul made plans for marriage.

The sixth month turned into the seventh month, and Miryam continued to take the serum, and was only seeing a little blood, but she was consciously getting more rest, spending more time in bed, which Saul did not find unusual. He continued to work, and stay close to home, turning down trips to Aela with more goods, for, as he explained to Alexander, Miryam was having difficulties with this pregnancy.

The day finally came in the seventh month when Miryam's water unexpectedly broke, and she sent Saul running to get Elizabeth, Wafi's wife. Elizabeth came on the run, as she had seen the devastation, both physical and emotional, a miscarriage causes in a patriarchal world where women are primarily valued as child-bearers, and in particular, bearers of sons. It had been so since the time of Abraham, and even before then in this fallen world. Saul stood by panic-stricken, holding the hand of his wife as she lay on the bed in agony, and praying, praying hard for divine intervention. But the bleeding just would not stop and then suddenly while Elizabeth was trying to calm Miryam, Miryam convulsed, screamed, and delivered a stillborn child and then the afterbirth. And still, the bleeding would not stop, no matter how many soft rags Elizabeth applied to area.

Suddenly, Elizabeth turned to Saul and said, "Run to the doctor's shop in the marketplace, ask for Anaximenes. This is beyond my skill level."

Frantic, Saul ran and was not sure which shop was the right one, and he began shouting in Greek, "where is the doctor, where is the doctor's shop?" Finally, after what seemed to be an eternity someone pointed him to the right door. He banged and banged on the door until an older man in a white toga came and said, "Yes? You are too early for the medicines." Saul with words pouring out of him explained what had happened and then quickly Anaximenes grabbed his bag, and came on the run, Saul fearing it was too late.

By the time Anaximenes arrived, Miryam was already very weak having lost a lot of blood, and she was slipping into unconsciousness whispering, "Where is my husband, where is my husband?" Saul knelt beside the bed and held Miryam's now quite cold hand. She whispered to him, "if I don't make it, I want you to know, I have accepted that Jesus is our Messiah, and have prayed for his help, as the great healer, in this hour."

Tears came gushing down Saul's cheeks and he said "Yes Jesus, *marana tha*, and help my poor Miryam."[1]

Anaximenes had been trained in the traditions of Hippocrates of Kos, and the first edict of that medical oath was, "Do no harm," and the second was, "Let the body heal itself." Nevertheless, in this case Anaximenes gave Miryam a sedative, and administered a sort of tourniquet procedure to stop the bleeding of the uterus. The procedure was successful, but the whole traumatic series of events left Miryam, who was a small woman with no extra body weight or margin for error, dangerously weak.

"She must be watched day and night," said Anaximenes. "There must be someone by her side constantly during this perilous period in her recovery. And most importantly, she must never get pregnant again. Never.

---

1. An Aramaic phrase used by Paul and other early Christians invoking the Lord to come, primarily in reference to the second coming. See 1 Cor 16.22.

Her body will not be able to take the strain. She will sleep now, all being well, for some hours, but watch her closely. If she stops breathing, pinch her nose and breath directly into her mouth, again and again, until she resumes breathing. And come get me if the bleeding resumes or she stops breathing."

Saul was shaking, on his knees holding his wife's cold hands and shaking. He barely was able to mumble a word of thanks to the doctor, and it was Elizabeth who walked the doctor out, and assured him she would make sure his instructions were executed to perfection. There followed a long sleepless night for Saul and Elizabeth, who stayed by Miryam's side like two watchdogs. Saul for his part was wracking his brain, and pleading with God, asking, "Is this because I haven't yet fulfilled my commission? Am I being punished for my delaying or doubting or uncertainties? Am I not to have the joys of having a family? Lord, I am your servant, and I know that you can work all things together for good, but I will not lay this disaster at your doorstep. I do not believe you do horrible things to loved ones, just to get us to do your will, and after all, it should have been me suffering not Miryam who had done no wrong in these matters. I leave my wife in your healing hands, as I am helpless to fix this problem. But I do hereby promise I will find a good way to bear witness to your Son Jesus, soon, whatever the personal cost."

Dawn came and Miryam was still sleeping, now less fitfully than during the previous evening. Her breathing seemed regular and normal. Elizabeth who had stayed right by Miryam's side said, "She will need some nourishment soon. I will go home now briefly, and fix us all some lentil soup, the soup Jacob once made for Esau." Saul smiled a weary smile and said *todah*, "thanks" in Hebrew.

About ten in the morning, Miryam began to stir, and moan, as she was still in great pain. Anaximenes had left a palliative to help with the pain, a draught of the opium poppy, though not a strong one. It was enough to dull the pain, not enough to knock the person out. Saul took a wooden spoon and gave Miryam some when she whispered "help." Within a half hour she was feeling less pain, and was able to open her eyes, and see her husband weeping by her side. She said, "I should have told you about my previous miscarriage, but I was afraid it would scare you off."

Saul replied, "It is you, Miryam, I fell in love with, not merely your child-bearing capacity, and it is you I still love today and am thankful you have survived."

At this juncture Elizabeth intervened and said, "You need something on your stomach more than just medicine. I've some lentil soup here and you must have some. You are very weak."

Slowly, Miryam rose up a little in her bed, and drank a surprising amount of soup. But then she lay back down and said, "I should sleep some more, so my body can recover."

The process of recovery took a long time. Indeed, it took over a month, and Saul and Elizabeth had to take turns watching Miryam. She had had a narrow escape from death. And it was not clear she would ever regain her full strength. If Saul had any hopes of Miryam traveling with him to share the Good News, those hopes faded fast. Very fast. So what was Saul to do with his commission? Time would tell. He now was a full two years from the day he left Jerusalem for Damascus, and no nearer to being the apostle to the Gentiles than on that day.

Death and Dying in the Ancient World

If anything is true about humans across the millennia, it is we all die and think about death and dying frequently. One might say the fear of death is the universal human experience. How we die and what we do after we die changes rapidly across time and space. Burial practices vary significantly from one culture to the next, and this much is true about the ancient world. The early Jesus movement was also profoundly interested in this ancient conversation about death and dying because at the center of their movement was their leader who had defied death. Jesus had been raised from the dead, and this had implications for the end of life for not just him, but everyone else. Although these views were not new or novel, they were rooted in the ancient beliefs of the Jewish faith, but the resurrection of Jesus transfigured them in important ways. These early Christian beliefs would have looked peculiar to many groups in the ancient world.

Greco-Roman Practices

Attitudes towards death varied in the ancient world among Greeks and Romans.[2] Perhaps most famously, the Greeks had a well-developed afterlife and philosophical approaches to the concept of life after death. The famous Elysian fields promised a blessed afterlife if one was one of the lucky few to attain it. Across a range of sources, what is evident is that when one dies,

---

2. *OCD*, 433–34 forms the basis of this chapter.

they lose their physical body and the terms that arise to describe the afterlife self are souls or shades. The domain of the dead was considered to be Hades. Depending on one's philosophical bent, the loss of the body was a good thing. Both Platonists and Stoics would heartily agree. There was undoubtedly a downgrade in the quality of existence in the afterlife. What was one to do with this reality? There are no clear answers from ancient sources. One can easily see why "eat drink for tomorrow we die" becomes a clarion call in the ancient world. Practices concerning the dead and their bodies also reflect this reality with cremation as the standard practice from 400 BC onward through the first century. Alongside cremation, some bodies were buried although there does not seem to be a religious belief differentiating between these practices. One's death was another opportunity to showcase one's status and wealth with elaborate bone boxes or *Sarcophagi* that came to dominate the ancient Greco-Roman world.

Romans continued, elaborated, and transformed many of these practices. The Greeks also shared a special meal on various dates. The Romans developed these practices with a meal not only on the day of the burial and the ninth day after death, but also on the anniversary of the deceased's funeral and then on their birthday as well. Various festivals, such as the *Paternalia* (February) and *Lemuria* (May) also commemorated all the dead in Rome. Remembering the dead included sacrifices on their behalf which were thought to not only appease the dead spirits but ensure their comfort as well. Perhaps most importantly, the sacrifices for the dead were a way of keeping their memory alive for "to be remembered was an important aspiration of the ancient world." Of course, as it is today, death involves not only a physical cost (the loss of life) but also a financial cost. For this reason, many poor persons in the ancient world would join collegia or associations, and with the paying of a small due, one of the responsibilities was the burial of the dead.

Jewish Burial Practices

Jewish burial practices, of course, differed from the pagan counterparts.[3] The afterlife in the Hebrew Bible was the place known as Sheol. There's a development of the afterlife in the Hebrew Bible moving towards a concept of resurrection. Most famously, texts like Ezek 37, Isa 26, and Dan 12 all begin to form a belief in a resurrected afterlife during the post-exilic period. What moves from a metaphorical resurrection of the nation in the earlier prophets comes to include individuals by the Persian period. Where resurrection makes strides is during the Second Temple period. The literature of this period interacts

---

3. Insights drawn from Collins, "Death and Afterlife," 524–46.

with the apocalyptic traditions(s) begun in the Hebrew bible. The book of Jubilees and some Enochic traditions attest to the resurrection, especially as it related to the apocalyptic judgment of the righteous and unrighteous. The Hellenistic period showcases a variety of beliefs. Some Jewish groups adopted Plato's theory on the immortality of the soul, most notably Philo and the Wisdom of Solomon. Some exceptions to this are the Maccabean literature and the Fourth Sibylline Oracle that advocate for a physical resurrection. As we move into the New Testament period, there is still no widespread agreement. In terms of Jesus' and Paul's contemporaries—the Pharisees were proponents of the resurrection, and most famously, the Sadducees were not. Hence the convoluted conversation in the Gospels on the "life to come" and the concept of marriage. The Early Jesus movement also provided much in terms of the development of the idea of resurrection primarily deriving from Jesus himself and the witnesses of his resurrection. Paul himself is a central advocate for the concept of a bodily resurrection in the afterlife with 1 Cor 15 being the crowning jewel of the argument. The resurrection of Jesus is the first fruits of the resurrection of all of God's people and becomes a source of hope in the present.

Burial practices for Jewish groups thus reflect the diversity of views on death and the afterlife.[4] Much of our information comes from excavated cemeteries in Jerusalem and Jericho. What appears common in the Second Temple period is tombs carved out of rock formations. These rock-tombs allowed one to enter and be fully upright once inside usually by having dug a pit into the floor. Jewish burials were performed in two stages. The first stage consisted of placing the body sometimes in a wooden, but at least into the rock-hewn, tomb. After decomposition, the bones would be exhumed and put into a bone box, called an ossuary. Depending on one's economic status, both the rock-hewn tombs and the ossuaries could be elaborately decorated. The individual bone box burials appear to increase as the belief in individual resurrection increases in the Second Temple period. The resurrection of Jesus, as depicted in the canonical gospels, reflects these ancient Jewish burial practices. The garden tomb is an example of the initial first stage of burial where the body would be prepared. Hence, the women bringing powerful and pungent spices to anoint the body, to ward off the odor for the week of visiting the tomb after the death. They would not come back for a year after that, because the flesh decayed slowly. Then they would disassemble the skeleton about a year later.

---

4. Drawn from Hachili, "Burial Practices," 448–52.

CHAPTER TWENTY-FIVE

A WINTER OF DISEASE AND DISCONTENT

Rats. Lots of rats. They had come into Petra via a caravan from Egypt, hiding in bags of grain. The ancients, largely ignorant of diseases that rats could carry and infect people with, nonetheless despised rats of all sorts. In the tenth month of the year (called the Decem month)[1] some sort of plague broke out in Petra, though even Anaximenes was not sure of the cause, though he suspected the rats had brought it with them. People began dying—infants, old people, the weak, the infirm, and Saul was very afraid for his Miryam so he kept their home ultra clean, and closed the business part of the shop, despite Miryam's protests.

Alexander, Saul's employer, watched helplessly as his wife of 40 years died of the plague. King Aretas held a special time of sacrifice to Atargatis asking that her healing power and mercy fall upon his people. But it did no good. It was at this juncture that he began looking around for scapegoats, and fastened on a theory, suggested by one of his Persian astrologer advisors, that the Jews living in Petra had caused this. Aretas was all too ready to believe this, in light of his recent dealings with the treacherous Herod Antipas. Thus he began to summon Jews before him to account for themselves. Had they brought this disease upon his Nabatean people. Could he stop the plague by banishing the Jews?

---

1. The Roman calendar had only ten months with our December which includes the Latin number ten, being the last. Notice October includes the number eight, November the number nine.

A WINTER OF DISEASE AND DISCONTENT

The day came that King Aretas summoned Saul of Tarsus to his court. Dressed in his finest robe, clean-shaven, he came into the court room where Aretas sat on his throne. "Saul of Tarsus, you are a recent inhabitant in our fair city, and you travel to Aela and elsewhere selling the wares of Alexander. Yes, I know of your activities. I wonder if you could have brought back from afar this horrible plague killing many of my peoples."

"Noble king Aretas, I am not the cause of this terrible trouble. Indeed, my friend and employer's own wife has recently died of it and I have watched in horror as this happened to many here in Petra. I would not wish this on anyone. I will say, good king, that there is a God whom I worship, we call him Jesus the Anointed One, who lived in my land of Israel, and healed many people. Perhaps, if all your people prayed to Him, he would intervene and help us stop this tragedy."

Aretas was angered: "You dare to suggest that our Nabatean gods are not powerful enough to heal us, who have served them so faithfully for so long?"

"Good king, I speak of only what I know. I know that people have been and are being healed in the name of Jesus, the risen Lord of heaven. If a man is drowning and the only person who throws him a rope and pulls him out of the sea is not one of his kind, should he say, 'I will not accept this help, since he is not one of my own'? That would not be wise. You believe in many gods, King Aretas, surely there is room for one more—named Jesus? But it is up to you."

"But you Jews do not believe in many gods, but only in your own god! Yes I know these things, and so I do not think you are sincere in suggesting I should simply believe in one more god, when in reality you would have me believe in none but your own god. Away with your false religion! I do not believe you come in peace and with healing from your god. I give you a week to pack your things, and leave town, and take this plague with you! If you do not, I will have you arrested and tried for the murder of many Nabateans!"

Saul stood shaking, bowed his head slightly, and left the court room with an armored guard. He stopped first at Alexander's shop to tell him the horrible news, and then went home. Home, only to find his wife Miryam had begun to have a fever, a very high fever indeed. Again the doctor was called, and again they used some opium and added some cold wet cloths to bring her fever down. And again, she was in danger. But this time there was no reprieve. This time the disease took over her weak body, and she passed away, with her final words to Saul being, "Do not blame yourself. Just know I have loved you, and now you must go everywhere Jesus the Lord wants you to go—sharing the good news about him. I trust I will see you in the next life, the everlasting life we have talked of." The next morning, as was the custom in Nabatea, Saul, Elizabeth, Wafi, and Alexander took Miryam's body on a funeral bier to the part of the necropolis where she could be buried. Saul said some prayers, thanked his friends for all their help, and explained he would be leaving the next day for Damascus. "I have only one day left before Aretas' men come for me, so I must leave in haste." At the end of the funeral ceremony, Saul went home, packed his things, and resolved to leave, heading north, first thing in the morning. He wondered what exactly had he accomplished in his two years and a bit in Petra. Certainly he had not yet become the "apostle to the Gentiles" as Jesus had intended. Now he would need to devote his life and all his energies to that task.

It was a cold winter's morning, with a stiff breeze coming down the narrow passage ways in Petra, as Saul saddled up the camel he had bought from Wafi, the one named Abraham. He packed his tools of the trade, his scrolls, especially the Isaiah scroll which he continued to study, and he wore the ring his wife had given him on the day of their wedding, a beautiful ring with a turquoise stone in it. He would never forget his happy days with Miryam. Saul did not look back as he left Petra, he simply pointed his camel up the spice road, and set his face like a flint towards an unknown future. He reflected on the story of Abraham, and how he moved on faith, not knowing where God would have him go before he set out for the promised land. Even Abraham the camel seemed to know more than Saul which way they would go next.

Getting Well: Medicine in the Ancient World

Archaeology has unearthed a treasure trove of ancient medical-related items. We have everything from medical instruments to the ancient version of a prescription pad. The ancient world, like our world, was concerned, as humanity is in general, with living and not dying. However, their understanding of health, disease, well-being, medicine, and death vary significantly from our modern conceptions. One initial impression gathered from the ancient evidence is that medicine was never a proper discipline in its own right, but was part of a broader philosophical approach. Alongside the physical evidence are the writings of Hippocrates and Galen that offer a courtside seat to a discussion of medical theory and practice. One should also not discount the role of Egypt in the medical developments of the ancient world and even further back, Babylonian traditions.[2] Galen wrote nearly three million words and produced introductory textbooks for aspiring physicians with works on such things as bones and pulses, anatomical texts, along with pharmaceutical texts.[3]

We must remember that much of ancient medicine was a mix of experimentation and trial by error. One was more likely to seek out a priest from a healing temple than to head to a physician. In a world before medical anesthesia, one understands the hesitation to "go under the knife" for a bodily ailment. Although we have access to medical textbooks, there does not appear to be any sort of official body to certify doctors or standardize treatment. By the first century, Cornelius Celsus had divided medical practice into three categories: nutrition, pharmacology, and surgery.[4] One was at the mercy of the physician's aptitude and technology available from place to place. Some practices ranged from the sane to the incredible. Some examples include mixing parts of a cow's brain with your food to make your eyelashes grow or binding a frog to a baby's head to help cure an infant's illness![5]

One must understand the relationship between medicine, disease, and the gods to understand the ancient conception of each. For example, the gods were known to send diseases against humanity as punishments. As such, the gods could also be appealed to for deliverance and healing. Salvation language in the ancient world often referred to physical restoration. To be "saved" was to be in good health or restored to good health. Healing temples consisted of three parts: a temple, a source of water such as a well or spring, and a room for sleeping known as an *abaton*. Some complexes were quite extensive, housing up to 160 people.[6] Magic also featured prominently, as magic was one means of manipulating a deity to do something on your behalf. Temples were filled with votives, incantation texts, and sacred objects. Snakes also featured prominently.

A center for medicine in the ancient world was the Greek island of Cos, home not only to for Hippocrates and his healing temple but also Asclepius, the patron deity of doctors and healing. Many doctors found training at Asklepieia at the temple of Asclepius. Cults to Asclepius are found throughout the ancient Mediterranean. Temples have been found in Athens, Corinth, and Rome, among others. Most training here would be more observational. The temple precincts were along the lines of a med-spa rather than

---

2. *OCD*, 945.

3. *OCD*, 949.

4. *OCD*, 946.

5. Cited in Keener, *Acts,* 1:418–19. Primary sources are Pliny the Elder, *Nat.* 29.37.115; 32.48.138.

6. Ferguson, *Backgrounds,* 224.

a medical complex. Patients would often spend the night. They would make plaster casts of various body parts that needed healing. More common was genitalia, as STDs were widespread in the ancient world. Problems seeking treatment might include everything from blindness, lameness, broken limbs, to baldness![7] Not all patients were admitted. If one was deemed too sick, one could be denied entry. Or if one took a turn for the worse, one could be kicked out and left in the woods to die. Death on the property was not good for business.

Contrary to modern expectations, doctors in the ancient world were not necessarily positions of social status as most doctors were slaves. Some of the more elite members of ancient society might have their own doctors. Julius Caesar had famously granted citizenship to doctors in Rome.[8] Doctors would travel from town to town, making "visits" (from which our word epidemic derives).[9] Some doctors could make considerable money if they were successful in both treatment and recruitment of patients. Generally, doctors were well respected among ancient people. Paul of course traveled with his co-partner, Luke the physician. One ought to look at the healing texts in the New Testament as part of this world and see the ways in which ancient persons would understand the God of Paul as the God who saves!

---

7. *OCD*, 946.

8. Suetonius, *Jul.* 42.1 cited in Keener, *Acts*, 1:420.

9. *OCD*, 946.

CHAPTER TWENTY-SIX

BACK TO DAMASCUS

THE JOURNEY BACK TO DAMASCUS PROVED TO BE LONGER THAN THE JOURney to Petra for the very good reason that the winds were howling from the north, and Saul had to travel against the wind. It took some twelve long days to get back to Damascus, and by the time he did, both he and Abraham the camel were completely worn out. What Saul could not know was that the plague had continued to strike down one Nabatean after another, and so Wafi and his wife had fled the city to Aela, and King Aretas decided that Saul had not taken the plague with him, so he wrote out a decree for his arrest. Learning that Saul had returned to Damascus, he had a courier take a message to his ethnarch in Damascus, one Nabad, to find Saul and return him to Petra for trial. But this would take some time, for Nabad had no idea what Saul looked like, and Saul, for his part had thought it wise to change his appearance once again—growing back his beard and moustache, and allowing his hair to grow as well. And in any case it was at least a dozen days' head start that Saul had on the courier.

Arriving in Damascus, Saul went immediately to Ananias' house. Ananias who now looked considerably older than when Saul had last seen him, was glad to see Saul and hear about his adventures and misadventures in Petra. He wept when he heard about Saul's loss of his child and his wife. After breaking bread together, Saul broached the question uppermost in his mind: "Do you think things have calmed down enough in Jerusalem for me to return there quietly, and consult with those now called the pillars of the new temple or assembly of God's people? I need to hear from them more about Jesus and his teachings, and frankly I reckon I want their endorsement for my mission, even though I was commissioned by Jesus himself, and could go on and do my mission without their endorsement?"

"Yes, I suppose you could do that," replied Ananias, stroking his grey and white beard, "but it would not be wise. There are too few Christ-followers in the world, there is already considerable opposition even from our own people, never mind the non-Jews, and so we must do our best to stick together, wouldn't you agree?"

"Indeed, I do, which is why I must go, but in this first instance, and since I have no Christ communities to report about, I will go and humbly ask to hear the story from Peter and others. It will be a learning and fact-finding trip, not a negotiation about legitimacy of a Gentile mission."

The two men continued to talk for many hours, and Ananias explained the difficulties of being a Christ-follower in Damascus, not only because of some opposition from some Jews, but also because a staunchly polytheistic ruler, Aretas, had gained control of the city, and as Saul already knew to his cost, was not tolerant of monotheistic claims about the Jewish god being the only true god.

Saul stayed with Ananias for a good two weeks, and was just beginning to relax when he heard the rumor that a courier from King Aretas had arrived in Damascus, and was consulting with Aretas' ethnarch, Nabad. "This does not augur well for you Saul," said Ananias. "We will need to slip you out of the city somehow, but I have just learned from my neighbors that they have locked all the city gates . . . but fear not, I have a plan." Ananias' plan was to put Saul in a laundry basket and lower him down the wall from a well-protected spot, not often patrolled by the authorities. Damascus was after all a large walled city, and not all of it would be watched all the time. Saul readily agreed with this plan, not least because his leaving would provide less danger for Ananias and the other Christ-followers in Damascus. He packed up his few belongings and told Ananias he was prepared whenever Ananias said was the appropriate hour.

BACK TO DAMASCUS

The traditional site where Saul is said to have been lowered down the city wall. Notice the Christian symbols, making clear this part of the wall was built much later than Saul's time as a memorial or pilgrimage spot.

Nabad was nothing if not vigilant, and he posted guards at every gate of the city.[1] But Ananias and his fellow Christ-followers had one of their number take Abraham the camel out of the city in broad daylight the day Saul was to leave, and tether him to a fig tree near the spot where Saul would be lowered down the wall.[2] While Saul was embarrassed and humbled by this exit, he knew it was necessary. Saul went down the road to Jerusalem with some fear and trepidation. Would he even be received by the Judean Christ-followers, or by their leaders? Many years later, Saul's sometime companion Luke would chronicle and summarize this part of Saul's story this way. "When he came to Jerusalem, he tried to join the disciples, but they were all afraid of him, not believing that he really was a disciple. But Barnabas took him and brought him to the apostles. He told them how Saul

---

1. Saul later said: "In Damascus the ethnarch of King Aretas had the city of the Damascenes guarded in order to arrest me. But I was lowered in a basket from a window in the wall and slipped through his hands." (1 Cor 11:32–33).

2. See also Acts 9:25.

on his journey had seen the Lord and that the Lord had spoken to him, and how in Damascus he had preached fearlessly in the name of Jesus. So Saul stayed with them and moved about freely in Jerusalem, speaking boldly in the name of the Lord. He talked and debated with the Hellenistic Jews, but they tried to kill him. When the believers learned of this, they took him down to Caesarea and sent him off to Tarsus" (Acts 9:26–30).

Approaching Jerusalem, Saul had mixed feelings. He was glad to be back in what had been the home of his youth, and he knew his sister would take him in, at least for a time. But how would Peter or James the brother of Jesus receive him? That would be far more crucial than how just any Christ-follower received him. At first Saul went to the Greek-speaking followers of Jesus, but they feared to let him in to their meeting, thinking he was pretending to be a follower of Jesus. But one of their number did believe Saul, and his name was Barnabas, a man from Cyprus. It was providential that Saul met him at this meeting, as Barnabas was to become his partner in mission some years later, and it was Barnabas who became the goodwill ambassador taking Saul to meet with the pillar apostles in private. It was now about three years since his conversion, and there were no converts to show for all his efforts in Petra, for his one true convert, Miryam, had died and could not attest to his work there.

CHAPTER TWENTY-SEVEN

THE "ROCK" MEETS THE MAN FROM ROCK CITY

"I did not go up to Jerusalem to see those who were apostles before I was, but I went into Arabia. Later I returned to Damascus. Then after three years, I went up to Jerusalem to get acquainted with Cephas and stayed with him fifteen days. I saw none of the other apostles—only James, the Lord's brother" (Gal 1:17–19).

The meeting was bound to be awkward. Despite Barnabas' assurances, and despite the written letter from Ananias in Damascus to the pillars on Saul's behalf, Cephas, as was his nickname given to him by Jesus himself, was suspicious and cautious. Saul had been a persecutor of Christ-followers, could he really have done a complete reversal and become one of them? It stretched credulity to the breaking point, but then, so did God's other miracles too. The purpose of the meeting, as far as Peter was concerned, was to make sure this man was not a spy, or traitor to the cause of Christ. But from Saul's point of view, he earnestly wanted to learn and understand the teachings and life of Jesus. He wanted to know the man Peter of course, but he wanted to know the story of Jesus' words and deeds even more urgently.

Things did not begin well, as Peter led off with accusations. "Why should I believe that Christ has accepted and changed and forgiven you, you who persecuted and even oversaw the stoning of our brother Stephanos more than three years ago now? Give me a reason?"

Instead, Saul replied, "Is it not true, as Ananias told me, that on the very night Jesus was betrayed by Judas, you also denied him three times after promising you would never forsake him? Is that story not true?"

This caught Peter by surprise. He was silent for a moment: "So you heard that story? Yes, I suppose you could say that there was a dramatic turning in my life too. And Jesus himself said to me at our last Passover meal: 'When you have turned back again, retrieve the others.' But if I had not seen the risen Lord after the crucifixion, I doubt we'd be here talking to each other on this day."

"As is true of me as well," volunteered Saul.

"Yet there is something very different about you," insisted Peter. "You did not see Jesus during the forty or so days he appeared to his disciples. Your revelation came much later, when Christ was in heaven. We saw him on earth, in the risen flesh, you did not, and besides you were an opponent, not a disciple or seeker of Jesus in a positive way."

"It is true I was like an *ektroma*, born out of due season into the following of Christ, but nonetheless it was the same risen Jesus whom I saw in my revelation."[1] Saul paused and wept for a moment, wiping tears from his eyes. The word *ektroma* had brought up the painful memory of Miryam's miscarriage. "But is it not true that Jesus' own brothers, including Jacob,[2] did not believe in Jesus until he appeared to them? Are they any different than me in that regard? They were also not his disciples."[3]

"You make a good point. Jesus did not just appear to his own previous disciples, or else Jacob would not be a leader here in Jerusalem of our movement even now."

"Tell me, I beg you," said Saul, "what was the essence of Jesus' teaching?"

Peter thought for a moment and said, "There were many facets to it, but at its very essence it was about loving God, and neighbor, and the stranger, and even one's enemies with one's whole heart. It was about always forgiving those who have sinned against you. It was about praying for those who persecute you, turning the other cheek when someone strikes you. It was about abandoning the use of violence to change people or the course of events. It was about being the servant of all, being self-sacrificial not self-centered. It was about being faithful to obey God, even to the point of martyrdom rather than betraying the Good News. It was about offering

---

1. See 1 Cor 15:8—an abortion or miscarriage, one born out of due season.
2. I.e., James.
3. John 7:5.

help, healing, change to not only the first, the most, and the found, but also to the last, the least, and the lost. It was about salvation, redemption for all peoples, all tribes, every ethnic group. It was about both men and women being equal in their discipleship and service to and witness for Jesus. It was not about perpetuating the same old fallen hierarchies of men over women, of free persons and masters over slaves, of one race over another. We were all in need of change, of redemption, which comes from the grace of our Lord Jesus."

Peter went on for several hours, recounting the story of Jesus from his baptism to his death and resurrection appearances. He told the story of how, quite unexpectedly, Jesus had appeared first to Miryam of Magdala and other women: "And they came and told us, but we thought it on old wives' tale, until we saw Jesus in person as well.[4] In many ways the story of the end of Jesus' life was not at all what we as Jews had expected of a messiah. We had not read Isaiah that way, for example."[5]

"Yes," interrupted Saul, "I have been studying my Isaiah scrolls diligently of late, and now reading it with new eyes, in light of the Good News story about Jesus. It's remarkable how much sense it makes of those poetic and puzzling prophecies. I gather then even Jesus' mother, Miryam, is a disciple now, and part of this Jerusalem community?"

"Yes, she is, as are the brothers and sisters of Jesus. It is an interesting mixture of previous and new disciples of the Lord Jesus."

"But so far, no Gentiles, right?"

"That's right, and I hear from Barnabas you seem to think you are called to bring them into our movement?"

"Exactly so. And I am hoping for the blessing of you and Jacob for such a mission."

"I cannot speak for Jacob, but as for me, I know I am simply called to share the Good News primarily with Jews, although I am open to others as well."[6]

The conversation continued for a full two weeks, and Saul was given some scrolls recounting the basic teaching of Jesus, and the last week of his life. Saul realized early on that Jesus' way of telling parables probably would

---

4. See Luke 24.

5. But as 1 Peter shows, Peter did come to read Isaiah that way.

6. On which see the Peter and Cornelius story in Acts 10. The question was—on what basis would Gentiles be accepted. Peter did not sort that out before he had his vision about visiting Cornelius. But already before then Philip had brought the Good News to Samaritans, who were not viewed as fully Jewish.

not be the best way to approach Gentiles in the Greco-Roman world.[7] Towards the end of all these intense and intensive sessions, Jacob finally came and met Saul. A man of small stature and apparently not very much like Jesus in appearance, Saul nonetheless sensed the fervor and kindness of the man.

"Saul, we welcome you into the followers of Christ," Jacob said, offering the right hand of welcome and fellowship. "Having consulted with Peter and John as well, we think it best—because the authorities here are still very much wanting to try you and incarcerate you, and also because many Christ-followers have not yet come to know the truth about you and still are afraid of you—if you leave right away. We are going to escort you to Caesarea Maritima, and ask you to go back to your home region, back to Tarsus, and start your proper mission there with genuine Gentiles. I gather the efforts in Arabia did not bear much fruit, not least because the Nabateans have their own culture and language. And I gather Aretas would still like to have you tried and convicted. In short, both here in Judea, and also in Damascus and the rest of Nabatean Arabia, you are too much of a wanted man, and you need a fresh start somewhere familiar, but well removed from where you've been recently."

This advice Saul had not anticipated, and he was about to object, when Jacob added, "Do not fear. We will be watching your progress in Tarsus, and in due course, we will send our friend Barnabas to find you, when things are well and truly much better and calmer than they are now. Godspeed, and may the Lord bless your ministry among the nations."

And so it was that, quite unexpectedly, Saul returned to the place of his birth. He could not know when he left Jerusalem that it would be another decade before he would see Barnabas' smiling face again.

---

7. In fact, there are no proper parables in Paul's letters, and only one real allegorizing of a historical story, in Gal 4, probably Paul's earliest letter.

CHAPTER TWENTY-EIGHT

RETURN TO CILICIA

HE FELT DISMISSED. HE FELT ENDORSED. HE TRIED TO UNDERSTAND WHAT had just happened from the point of view of the fears of the Christians in Judea. He decided finally, as he was boarding a boat in Caesarea Maritima, to accept that he was *persona non grata*, and he was endangering the fragile movement if he stayed in Jerusalem. He might even be found and incarcerated by the temple police who worked for the high priest. He must look to the future, and the future involved no more entangling alliances, marriages, or relationships with patrons that restricted his mobility. He had a divinely appointed task to fulfill, and he would do it, come what may. So, on to Tarsus, but it hardly felt like a trip home. After all, his family had left there long ago.

The city had a long history, even involving Antony and Cleopatra who once visited, which produced a ceremonial city gate for which the city had become famous.

Cleopatra's City Arch

Saul wracked his brains as to which of his relatives might be still living in Tarsus. After all, he had left that city when he was about 10, and that was decades ago. There might be an uncle or an aunt that still lived in Tarsus, but Saul hardly thought they would even recognize him, never mind take him in. Once again, he was solitary, a man alone, except for his God. And *that* God nobody in Tarsus had yet embraced.

When he first walked into the city through the city gate, nothing much had seemed to change, except that through the emperor's patronage there was now a Cardo Maximus or main street running straight through the middle of the city.

RETURN TO CILICIA

This is in fact a reconstruction of what the cardo looked like in Jerusalem in Paul's day. The one in Tarsus would have looked much the same.

The remains of the Cardo in Tarsus today.

There were lots of shops on both sides of the street, and trading seemed to be brisk. Saul remembered where the synagogue was in Tarsus, and reckoned he could make a start there with the sharing of the good news. After all, the good news about a Jewish messiah was indeed for the Jew first, and also for the Gentile. He passed the place where his father's leather-working shop had once been, but now it was a potter's work shop, where all sorts of amphorae, clay lamps, cooking pots, and much more was being made. He would need to find a place where he could return to his trade. The Roman legion was still decamped outside of Tarsus as the main force supervising the province of Syria/Cilicia, and he expected they still needed more leather products, including tents.

After the long walk through town, he turned to the *subura*[1] area of the city, where there were high-rise tenement buildings. Saul reflected on the history of his town as he walked along. It was Pompey, some 50 or more years before he was born, who subjugated this city to the Romans after he had crushed the Cicilian pirates who had sailed down the Cydnus river and had terrorized the sea trade until Julius Caesar and Pompey had put an end to all that. Before that, Alexander the Great had passed through this city, and nearly died in Tarsus, after bathing in the Cydnus river. There was an old saying: "We used to say, if you drink from the Cydnus you will always return. Now we say if you drink from the Cydnus, you will never leave," referring to the refuse and vermin that clogged up the river in the first century.[2]

All the way back to the time of the Persian occupation, Tarsus had been a major city, ruled by a client king of Cyrus at one point. By the time of Augustus, Tarsus had become a major intellectual center, like Athens, with its own famous Greek Academy. In fact, the first tutor of Octavian (or Augustus) had been Athenodorus a famous philosopher from Tarsus. Tarsus had a long and proud intellectual history. It was because of Athenodorus' relationship with Augustus that the city continued in the patronage and good graces of the Roman emperors during the entire lifetime of Saul.

Saul finally arrived at a familiar-looking building where he had once lived. He doubted any of his relatives were still there, but still . . . it was worth the effort to find out. He knocked gently on the door of the first floor apartment, and a very elderly lady with long gray hair open the door a crack and said, "Yes, who is it? What do you want?"

---

1. The *subura* was a term first used to refer to high-rise apartment structures in the poorer part of Rome. It is the word from which we got the term suburb. It came to be applied to any high-rise apartment structures in the major cities of the empire.

2. This proverb actually was used to refer to the polluted Nile in the first place.

"I am Saul of Tarsus, returned to my hometown, and I was trying to find members of my extended family." The door opened wide, as did the eyes of the old lady who responded, "Saul, can that really be you after so many years? You will not recognize me but I am your aunt Sarah! Please come in."

Saul flashed back in his mind to his childhood, playing in the streets here with his cousin Marcus, the son of Sarah. Before he had even a moment to say any more he was greeted and welcomed by several of his relatives. Sarah explained, "Marcus is down in the cardo working away at our leather shop, no not the one your father once owned, but close to it. He will be thrilled to see you. Welcome home! There is a little apartment in this block you could rent and be close to family. We must hear your story about becoming a scholar in Jerusalem and how the rest of the family is doing there."

It was clear to Saul that no one here had heard the news about his persecuting Christ-followers or his being wanted by the Sanhedrin, much less his flight to Arabia and return to Damascus. Saul was thankful that was the case. Perhaps he really could make a fresh start here in Tarsus.

The rest of the day was taken up with family meetings and catching up. Saul decided to tell the part of the story about how he had moved to Petra, worked as a tentmaker, had gotten married, and lost both his child to miscarriage, and his wife to some sort of plague or pestilence. He finished his story, saying, "so I have come home to make a fresh start. My parents have both been gathered to our ancestors sometime ago and only my sister and her son still live in Jerusalem, a city in constant difficulties."

"We are glad you are home. We must have a big meal together tonight to celebrate. Perhaps you can become a tutor in the Academy, or in the Torah study house at the synagogue. Certainly, you can come help us in the leather-working business. Marcus can use another steady hand for sure."

Perhaps, thought Saul, his life really had fallen in good places—finally. Perhaps he could find a non-polemical way of sharing the good news in his hometown. And so for the next several years of his life, Saul worked hard in Marcus' shop, occasionally he debated with the philosophers in the Academy in a friendly way. Most of them thought the very idea of a resurrected person was absurd. Occasionally he would preach in the synagogue, alluding to the promised messiah, and the prophecies of Isaiah. He reasoned with the teachers in the Torah study building adjacent to the synagogue that messiah could have already come, but none of this produced any fruit, any converts. It simply branded Saul as a strange Jew with strange ideas. And this went on for years.

Saul had begun to wonder whether he would ever hear from the apostles in Jerusalem, would he ever be summoned to meet again with them. Had they simply abandoned him? But then came a day when, quite unexpectedly, he had another vision. He had begun to keep a journal and he later reflected on this vision as follows:

"I will go on to visions and revelations from the Lord. I know a man in Christ who fourteen years ago was caught up to the third heaven. Whether it was in the body or out of the body I do not know—God knows. And I know that this man—whether in the body or apart from the body I do not know, but God knows—was caught up to paradise and heard inexpressible things, things that no one is permitted to tell. I will boast about a man like that, but I will not boast about myself, except about my weaknesses. Even if I should choose to boast, I would not be a fool, because I would be speaking the truth. But I refrain, so no one will think more of me than is warranted by what I do or say, or because of these surpassingly great revelations. Therefore, in order to keep me from becoming conceited, I was given a stake in my flesh, a messenger of Satan, to torment me. Three times I pleaded with the Lord to take it away from me. But he said to me, "My grace is sufficient for you, for my power is made perfect in weakness." Therefore, I will boast all the more gladly about my weaknesses, so that Christ's power may rest on me. That is why, for Christ's sake, I delight in weaknesses, in insults, in hardships, in persecutions, in difficulties. For when I am weak, then I am strong."[3]

The vision reassured Saul that God still had plans for his life, but the stake or thorn in his flesh was a problem that had gotten worse as time went on, namely his partial blindness and the pain and tearing up of his eyes, which had been a problem off and on since his Damascus Road experience. It was difficult to do precise sowing work when one's eyes were constantly bothering one. Saul did not share this vision with his family members. He wanted to maintain good relationswith them, and so he continued to work.

In the Academy, Saul had met and befriended a young Greek named Titus. Saul had success in convincing this God-fearer, that the God of the Bible had sent forth his son Jesus to save both Jews and Gentiles alike. And

---

3. 2 Cor 12:1–10. This vision clearly happened during "the hidden years." If we date 2 Corinthians to the early to mid-50s, then this vision happened sometime in the early 40s, before Paul's first missionary journey.

RETURN TO CILICIA

so began a considerable period of discipling of Titus in the good news, sharing the prophecies with him that were relevant to explaining a messiah who suffered and atoned for the sins of everyone. Titus was in his twenties, and was very bright.

He soaked up the learning that Saul offered him like a sponge, and the two spent many hours together in prayer and study. *Finally*, Saul felt like he was fulfilling his commission.

But a day came when he had been asked to reflect on the scriptures and speak in the synagogue, and he believed it was time finally to be a bit bolder in sharing the good news. Little did he know that there would be a special guest listening in the synagogue on that Sabbath—one Barnabas of Cyprus.

CHAPTER TWENTY-NINE

THE SYNAGOGUE SERMON

SAUL MUSTERED UP HIS COURAGE, PUT ON HIS BEST TOGA, AND PREPARED to go and share from the Scriptures about the Jesus whom he served. He realized this could result in rejection, even by his family, indeed it could even result in him having to endure the forty lashes minus one for false teaching. At this point he did not care. He was frustrated that he had had so few converts to the following of Christ. On this Sabbath there was a good crowd in the synagogue, including members of Saul's own extended family. Saul did not notice the man with the long beard standing in the back, because his vision wasn't good on this day. The synagogue president read from the Scriptures that Saul had requested, and then Saul stood up, lifted up his hand for silence, said a prayer and began . . .

"'Fellow Israelites and you Gentiles who worship God, listen to me! The God of the people of Israel chose our ancestors; he made the people prosper during their stay in Egypt; with mighty power he led them out of that country; for about forty years he endured their conduct in the wilderness; and he overthrew seven nations in Canaan, giving their land to his people as their inheritance. All this took about 450 years.

"After this, God gave them judges until the time of Samuel the prophet. Then the people asked for a king, and he gave them Saul son of Kish, of the tribe of Benjamin, who ruled forty years. After removing Saul, he made David their king. God testified concerning him: 'I have found David son of Jesse, a man after my own heart; he will do everything I want him to do.'

"From this man's descendants God has brought to Israel the Savior Jesus, as he promised. Before the coming of Jesus, John preached repentance

THE SYNAGOGUE SERMON

and baptism to all the people of Israel. As John was completing his work, he said: 'Who do you suppose I am? I am not the one you are looking for. But there is one coming after me whose sandals I am not worthy to untie.'

"Fellow children of Abraham and you God-fearing Gentiles, it is to us that this message of salvation has been sent. The people of Jerusalem and their rulers did not recognize Jesus, yet in condemning him they fulfilled the words of the prophets that are read every Sabbath. Though they found no proper ground for a death sentence, they asked Pilate to have him executed. [29] When they had carried out all that was written about him, they took him down from the cross and laid him in a tomb. But God raised him from the dead, [31] and for many days he was seen by those who had traveled with him from Galilee to Jerusalem. They are now his witnesses to our people.

"We tell you the good news: What God promised our ancestors he has fulfilled for us, their children, by raising up Jesus. As it is written in the second Psalm:

"'You are my son;
today I have become your father.'

God raised him from the dead so that he will never be subject to decay. As God has said,

"'I will give you the holy and sure blessings promised to David.'

So it is also stated elsewhere:

"'You will not let your holy one see decay.'

"Now when David had served God's purpose in his own generation, he fell asleep; he was buried with his ancestors and his body decayed. But the one whom God raised from the dead did not see decay.

"Therefore, my friends, I want you to know that through Jesus the forgiveness of sins is proclaimed to you. Through him everyone who believes is set free from *every sin*, a justification you were not able to obtain under the law of Moses. Take care that what the prophets have said does not happen to you:

"'Look, you scoffers,
wonder and perish,
for I am going to do something in your days
that you would never believe,
even if someone told you.'"[1]

---

1. This is Luke's sermon summary of what Paul preached in the synagogue in Pisidian Antioch, found in Acts 13. But it would have been something quite like this that he

When Saul finished his message, there was a stirring in the congregation. Some reacted in a strongly negative way—"What is this man saying? That a crucified manual worker from Galilee is our messiah? The man should not be allowed to speak again, indeed some of what he has said is surely blasphemy, he should be dragged out and whipped and caused to repent." And indeed, before Saul knew quite what was happening, he was dragged out and whipped thirty-nine times with a leather strap while his family, Titus, and Barnabas stood aghast at what was happening.[2]

When the whipping was over, and the elders left Saul on the ground, Barnabas and Titus—not members of his own family who were ashamed of what had happened and who did not want further shame to come upon the family—came to him. Titus had gotten some water from the nearby cistern and a cloth, and Barnabas had a little anointing oil to administer to the welts on Saul's back. Saul was still conscious, and when he was rolled over on his side, he looked up, and there not six inches from his face he saw someone he finally recognized—"Barnabas, is that you?"

"Yes Saul, it's me your old friend Barnabas. I am sending Titus to collect your things. God is doing great things in Antioch on the Orontes, and we need your help. Many Gentiles have come to the Lord there, and I have not forgotten your commission. I believe you can be a great help. The citizens of Antioch have noticed the growth of our sect and have given us a name *christianoi*—partisans of Christ. I like it. But it is clear you have no more ministry here. It will just result in more agony for you. So, you and Titus must come with me to Antioch. There is much to be done!"

Saul smiled through the pain and said, "I thought you all had abandoned me. But I am very glad you are here on this day, and yes, I will go with you and see this thing the Lord is doing in Antioch. Perhaps I can help." So once again, the man without a family, no longer advancing in Judaism, was on the move again.

---

would have shared in Tarsus, if he had been invited to do so.

2. Paul says in 2 Cor 11:24–25: "Five times I received from the Jews the forty lashes minus one. Three times I was beaten with rods, once I was pelted with stones, three times I was shipwrecked, I spent a night and a day in the open sea." Some of this surely happened during the hidden years that this novel covers, and since he was in Cilicia for a long period before Barnabas came for him, it is likely this happened at least once to him while preaching in the synagogue there, thereby having a similar experience to Jesus when he preached in his hometown synagogue in Nazareth.

CHAPTER THIRTY

ANTIOCH ON THE ORONTES

Like Tarsus, Antioch was an ancient and important city. The city had been founded by one of Alexander the Great's generals, one Seleucus I, Nicator. Its location, at the place where the Silk Road, the Spice Road, and the Royal Road all converged, made it a major hub of business and commercial activity. At one point so prosperous was the city that it rivaled Alexandria as the greatest city in the eastern end of the Mediterranean crescent. The Romans made it the seat of government for the province of Cilicia. It also became a major center of Hellenized Judaism, of the very sort Saul had been raised in, Tarsus. It was the Septuagint that was read in the synagogues there, the version Saul knew best. Here Jews and Gentiles mingled freely, and here the edicts of tolerance prevailed, such that friendships between Jews and Gentiles were not uncommon, and meals were even shared between the two ethnic groups of people.

Saul had never visited Antioch, but had heard much about the city all his life. Its fame had spread far and wide. It was a city of some 250,000 at the time Saul was born, making it one of the 4–5 largest cities in the Roman Empire. It was not difficult to get lost in the crowds in this city.

The journey from Tarsus to Antioch was an arduous one, especially for Saul who was still healing from his wounds and bruises. It was some 85 Roman miles and he and Barnabas and Titus took it slow, for Saul's sake. Plus, it required passing through the Cilician gates, a high mountain pass that involved an arduous climb. By the time they arrived in Antioch, a week had passed, and Saul was exhausted when they got there. Some days of rest followed before Saul was fit to meet with the *christianoi* in the city, and find out what was happening. There were a variety of household meetings of Jewish and Gentile followers of Jesus, and Saul wanted to visit them all, which would take some time. But Saul was in no hurry. He figured he might be in Antioch for a considerable period of time, now that he had support of both Barnabas and Titus.[1]

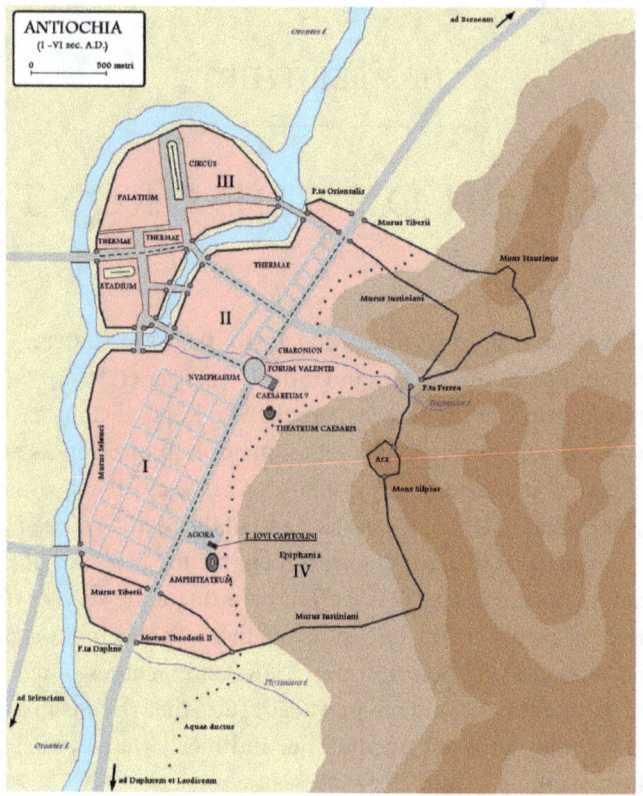

Schematic of first-century Antioch

What was apparent to Saul, was that there was no central organization to the Christ-follower meetings in Antioch. It was catch as catch can, and one of the reasons Barnabas fervently wanted Saul to come to Antioch was to help with the unifying and structuring of the body of believers there. One of the fruits of Hellenism in Antioch, is that most Jews had a more relaxed view of table fellowship with Gentiles than was the case in Jerusalem

---

1. One of the great mysteries of the Book of Acts is why Titus never appears in any of the narratives. This has even led to the speculation that Titus was the author of the book, but the evidence favors Luke, the beloved physician.

or even Damascus. They figured they could always do the rites of ritual purification after a meal with Gentiles, if their conscience bothered them about being in an unclean house, and possibly even eating some unclean food, though most of them politely refused to consume pork or shellfish, even in a Gentile household.

Without realizing it, the Antioch church was modeling how Jew and Gentile could be unified in Christ without compromising their faith. Yes, there would have to be concessions on both sides to some extent, but what was more important was the unity of the movement and its growth. The sharing of the Lord's Supper was an important unifying factor.

After spending some months in Antioch, Saul realized that what was happening *de facto* in Antioch needed to be thought through theologically. And so it was that Saul came to the conviction that the new covenant must be a genuinely *new* covenant, not a renewal of the Mosaic one, or merely a fulfillment of the heart of the Mosaic Law about loving God and neighbor. Saul realized that Jesus' teachings in some respects not only went beyond the Mosaic law and intensified, but in some cases nullified various Mosaic permissions—for example permission to divorce, and permission to use oaths and permission to use a limited amount of violence to solve problems. At one point Saul wrote down some of his thoughts about these things:

> Love must be sincere. Hate what is evil; cling to what is good. Be devoted to one another in love. Honor one another above yourselves. Never be lacking in zeal, but keep your spiritual fervor, serving the Lord. Be joyful in hope, patient in affliction, faithful in prayer. Share with the Lord's people who are in need. Practice hospitality.
>
> Bless those who persecute you; bless and do not curse. Rejoice with those who rejoice; mourn with those who mourn. Live in harmony with one another. Do not be proud, but be willing to associate with people of low position. Do not be conceited.
>
> Do not repay anyone evil for evil. Be careful to do what is right in the eyes of everyone. If it is possible, as far as it depends on you, live at peace with everyone. Do not take revenge, my dear friends, but leave room for God's wrath, for it is written: "It is mine to avenge; I will repay," says the Lord. On the contrary: "If your enemy is hungry, feed him; if he is thirsty, give him something to drink. In doing this, you will heap burning coals on his head."
>
> Do not be overcome by evil, but overcome evil with good . . .

> Let no debt remain outstanding, except the continuing debt to love one another, for whoever loves others has fulfilled the law. The commandments, "You shall not commit adultery," "You shall not murder," "You shall not steal," "You shall not covet," and whatever other command there may be, are summed up in this one command: "Love your neighbor as yourself." Love does no harm to a neighbor. Therefore love is the fulfillment of the law.[2]

All along, Saul realized that Sabbath laws, food laws, and the practice of circumcision were the practices which most defined the boundaries of Judaism, and kept Jews separate from Gentiles in various ways. Saul concluded that in the new covenant these rules became obsolete, and indeed there was even a new covenant sign that was gender inclusive—baptism instead of circumcision.

Eventually, Saul also came to the conclusion that the new covenant could be viewed as the fulfillment of the Abrahamic covenant, and that meant that the Mosaic covenant had to be seen as an *interim* arrangement until Messiah came to inaugurate the eschatological change of the ages and the new covenant. The Mosaic law acted as a child-minder of God's people until the time had come for Messiah to redeem his people out from under the yoke of that Law.[3] Christ had fulfilled and brought to a conclusion the Mosaic covenant and through his death, resurrection, and Spirit giving, had started the new and final covenant, involving Jew and Gentile united in Christ. It was not enough to incorporate Gentiles into Judaism—they both needed to be baptized into the new body of Christ on equal terms. In Christ, there could be no Jew and Gentile separation. All must be one in Him.

But the difficulty with being a global thinker who is the first one who works out logically the implications of a new belief system is that others did not immediately realize these implications, and some would clearly reject them, as Saul would soon learn to his regret. He discussed these things with Barnabas who seemed to be persuaded of what Paul was articulating, and Titus who more whole-heartedly accepted Paul's views.

There came a day when Saul realized he needed to go to Jerusalem and present his version of the good news. Indeed, he had vision one night

---

2. Selections from Rom 12–13.
3. This is exactly the argument we find in Paul's earliest letter—in Gal 4.

telling him he must go and he felt Barnabas and Titus must come as well and tell the pillars what God was doing in Antioch.[4]

Once the message came back from Jerusalem saying yes, there should be a private meeting with the pillars about these crucial matters. But that required a walk of over 300 Roman miles, no small journey, and one that would take the three men through Damascus, something Saul thought was not wise to do. So instead they caught a boat from Antioch down the Orontes to the sea, and from thence on to Caesarea Maritima. They walked the remainder of the journey to Jerusalem. Saul hoped that this visit would not turn out the same way the last one had.

---

4. Gal 2:1–2—"Then after fourteen years, I went up again to Jerusalem, this time with Barnabas. I took Titus along also. I went in response to a revelation."

CHAPTER THIRTY-ONE

THE SECOND RETURN TO ZION

It was a nice spring day in Jerusalem and the fig and olive trees were beginning to bud out.

The cool refreshing and light breeze felt like a nice welcoming back to the city Saul loved, but also feared. Barnabas had some business to attend to in the city, wanting to visit with his nephew, John Mark, and so Titus and Saul were the ones knocking on Saul's sister's door, this bright morning.

"Shalom alechem!" said Saul, "can you recognize me?" So startled was Deborah that she dropped the little pottery lamp she had in her hand, and it shattered on the limestone floor. "Oh bother! I'll clean that up later. Come in, brother, come in, and introduce me to your friend." Saul noticed that she was wearing the jewelry he had sent her from Miryam's shop in Petra.

"This is my understudy Titus, from Tarsus. I've come to town for a meeting, so I won't be here long but I did not want to neglect my brotherly duty and see you." And with this he embraced his sister and gave her a holy kiss on the cheek. "You look wonderful, you've hardly aged. As for me, the story is different."

Deborah cleared away some things, and the three of them sat and talked for what must have been the better part of two hours. She brought some bread and olives and small wine cups for them while they conversed. "So you did get married? I was worried that would never happen, but I am so sorry how that all ended. You must have been heartbroken."

"I certainly was, losing both my wife and my child in a very short span of time. I am now located in Antioch, and things are going well there, so I expect to stay there for some time to come. What about you?"

"As you may have deduced, we have a new high priest, still another relative of Annas, and they finally gave up their manhunt for you, thank goodness. I got tired of them repeatedly banging on my door and asking if you had showed up and if I knew where exactly you were. Which of course I didn't, so I didn't have to tell any false tales. If I were you, I would not put in an appearance in the temple courts, but just go to your private meeting, which you say is in Bethany, and then return to Antioch. It will be safer all around. As for me and things in Jerusalem, I still work at Jacob's pottery shop, sanding and glazing and polishing things. My days are all much the same, although you would be proud of your nephew David he is becoming a scholar like you."[1]

"Excellent, and I entirely agree with your advice," said Saul, "but I wanted you to know I was alive and still cared about my family here. I hope on some future trip we will be able to have a proper visit."

"May it be soon, and may your meeting be for a blessing to all."

"Yes," sighed Saul, "I hope I don't have to do too much arguing."

---

1. It was this nephew that was to come to his rescue many years later when Paul spoke in the temple courts in Jerusalem, causing a near riot. See Acts 23:16–17.

"Which you are too prone to do."
"Which I am indeed too prone to do. Shalom sister, be well."

CHAPTER THIRTY-TWO

THE SECRET MEETING

SAUL, BARNABAS, TITUS, AND BARNABAS' COUSIN, JOHN MARK, ALL CAME to the crucial meeting, which was also attended by Cephas, Jacob, John, and a few others whom Saul did not know. Initially Jacob told these others that they should not be present, but they argued with Jacob and finally won him over. They were Pharisaic followers of Jesus and wanted to hear from this controversial figure named Saul the former Pharisee. The meeting room was small, an upper room in the house of Mary, Martha, and Lazarus in Bethany. There would be no disturbances, and the host family stayed downstairs during the meeting.

After initial greetings and identifications of everyone, Jacob asked Saul to speak, and it became apparent to Saul that Jacob, and not Cephas, surprisingly, was the leader and host of this meeting.

Saul stood up in the middle of the room, raised his hand as a rhetorician would and began to speak. "I have come here to lay before the Jerusalem leaders of our movement, the message I have been preaching and sharing for some years now, lest I be running in vain. I have my Gospel from Christ himself, who is also the person who called me to be his servant, his messenger, so I am not asking for a commission from you, but I think it vital that we all be in agreement on the basis of which Jews and Gentiles can participate together in this Christ movement.

"I have come to the position I am about to articulate through agonizing experiences, even including physical abuse by my fellow Jews, but this has only strengthened me in my conviction that the Gospel must be offered to Gentiles without insisting on their dependence or acceptance of the whole Mosaic Law. Jesus came to inaugurate a new covenant, which is not simply a renewal of the Mosaic covenant, but rather is a genuinely new covenant, fulfilling the heart of the Mosaic covenant but also adding to it the new teachings of Christ, which in various cases replace or make obsolete what Moses said, due to the hardness of our hearts. For instance, Jesus said no oath taking, he said no divorce, except in cases where a relationship was not a marriage in God's eyes in the first place, as in the incestuous relationship between Herod Antipas and Herodias. Perhaps most importantly, Christ called us to always forgive, to never use violence on anyone for any reason, and even to love our enemies. This is a message that goes well beyond Moses and in some cases nullifies the Mosaic permissions due to hardness of heart. Jesus spoke to these matters. He even said 'it is not what enters a person that defiles them but what comes out of their hearts.'[1]

"I take this to mean that the new covenant does not require Gentiles to submit to circumcision and the 613 commandments of the Mosaic Law. But this in turn means that our movement cannot simply be seen as yet another sect of Judaism. If Jew and Gentile are to be united in Christ, it must be on the basis of the good news about Jesus and the new covenant, not on the basis of the Mosaic Law. In short, Jesus was calling us to the final, eschatological form of biblical faith, grounded in the new covenant. Initial salvation is by grace through faith in the Gospel of Jesus. It does not come merely through recognizing God chose us in the Exodus and Sinai events and us responding through covenantal nomism, and faithfulness to the Mosaic Law. The new people of God are Jew and Gentile united through faith in the Gospel. And the evidence that this new eschatological situation has come to pass is standing right before you in the person of Titus, who has been redeemed by Christ, and is as true a follower of our Biblical God as anyone standing here."

At this juncture, one of the Pharisaic Jews present named Phineas burst out angrily, "You would require no circumcision of the heathens? We have sat with him in violation of our Mosaic customs. Let him be circumcised and keep the Law which is an eternal law. He must first become a Jew in order to be a true follower of the Jewish messiah Jesus!"

Saul took a deep breath, and said, "You do not understand that we are all entering this religion on the basis of grace and through faith in Christ who has redeemed us, and the sign of our new covenant is baptism, not circumcision. If you change the covenant sign, you've changed covenants.

---

1. See Mark 7:15.

The new covenant is profoundly connected to the Abrahamic one—as the Scripture says, 'Abraham trusted God, and it was credited to him as right standing with God.' Abraham came before Moses, and he received right standing with God before he was ever circumcised. And he never knew all the strictures of the Mosaic Law nor did he have to keep them to have right standing with God. He was justified before God by grace and through faith, just as we are, just as Titus is."

Another of the Pharisaic believers asked, in a strong voice, "So then are you saying we Jews should abandon our traditions and customs we have learned from Moses?"

Saul replied, "I am saying that you may continue to keep those laws, especially as a way to be the Jew to the Jew to be a good witness to them, but this is no longer required of you. It can be a blessed option, especially if you want to reach Jews with the good news, but it is not required even of us Jews, for now the heart of the matter is that we are *christianoi* as we are called in Antioch, partisans of Christ. So it is, that I can be the Jew to the Jew to win some, but I can also be the Gentile to the Gentile when it comes to matters of food, or Sabbath-keeping or circumcision—those boundary definers which fence us off from Gentiles. If we can agree that the Mosaic covenant should not be imposed on the Gentiles, that will be the first step in the right direction."

It was clear from the heated discussion that ensued that Saul had stirred up yet another hornet's nest, and the Pharisaic Jewish followers of Jesus did not agree with Saul about the obsolescence of the Mosaic covenant. Jacob also had reservations about this, but said he would think more on the matter. Cephas was inclined to agree with Saul having himself had visions that led him to the house of a Roman soldier Cornelius, whom he shared the Gospel with and baptized. And Cephas spoke up in strong terms about Saul being a legitimate called apostle of Christ to the Gentiles, just as he was an apostle primarily to Jews. The pillars agreed to recognize the legitimacy of Saul's mission and preaching to Gentiles, since Jesus himself had said to make disciples of all the nations. The one stricture Jacob asked of Saul was to take up a collection for the Jerusalem saints, many of whom were living in poverty, and were banned from the dole, because followers of Jesus were not on the approved list of widows and orphans and others needing help. In addition, there was the problem of the food shortage caused by periodic famines in Egypt. Saul promised he would do his best to raise money for that cause as he began his mission to the Gentiles. The meeting ended with

Saul being given the right hand of fellowship, and being told they thought his apostleship was genuine. Yet it was not to be the Jerusalem church that commissioned Paul's first genuine missionary venture—it was the Antioch church.

Ancient Religion

Religion was a fundamental feature of the Greco-Roman world. Everyone was religious to some extent. Polytheism was the name of the game, and hence everyone believed in a god or multiple gods. There were some philosophers, like Cicero, who made negative comments on the proliferation of the numbers of gods—"are there really that many?" But the existence of deities was taken for granted. Most of human history has held a belief in a divine being/s. The modern enlightened world is a rare exception and represents a tiny dot on the timeline of human history. Perhaps there is much to learn from the ancients here. There was a deity that governed every aspect of human life; this included one's home, one's vocation, your well-being, to the ruler of the empire himself. One ought to pay attention to the gods as to disregard them would be to invite their wrath. What was well known was that the gods were vindictive and would lash out, so best to keep them happy. One of the more popular features of the ancient religious world is that the gods are wrathful. Rom 1:18 would not have been surprising from an ancient viewpoint; more surprising would have been the gracious and merciful aspects of Yahweh towards humanity.

Although religion was a piece of ancient reality, not all gods are worshiped in the same way. Some fundamental features do stand out. To be a "religion" in the ancient world, one needed to have a temple, priests, and sacrifices. One immediately notices two things. First, ancient Judaism adheres to this ancient model. Second, this is what makes the early Christians especially peculiar. They want to be treated like a religion in the ancient world but bear none of the typical feature, i.e., no priests, temples, or literal sacrifices. Ancient Romans may have scratched their heads in confusion at the request to be viewed as a religion.

Greek and Roman gods had homes, or what we call temples or a sacred place. The temple was their base of operations, and although gods could be worshiped throughout the empire, they had a special relationship to specific locations. Like the ancient version of a sports team, ancient deities had "home turf" and were thought to be more powerful there than anywhere else. We see this, for example, in the book of Acts and the worship of Artemis in Ephesus. Within these sacred places were sacred activities, such as prayer and sacrifice. How would one know what to pray or do in the temple? Here are where priests or sacred orders would come into play. The priests would be in charge of the running of temples and orchestrating the lives of the worshipers. The priests would primarily be in charge of teaching the prayers with the specific words and right intonations of voice. Likewise, they would help run the sacrificial cult and the slaughter of animals. Now that we have some fundamental features of ancient Roman religion in place (priests, temples, sacrifices), we can now talk about some key components of religious life.

Two key terms focus the conversation on ancient religion: *pietas* and *religio*. As a worshiper approaches a temple, they would be concerned with *pietas*. The term *pietas* referred to the degree to which one followed the priests' instructions or rites most closely and doing one's obligations to the deity or deities. The term *pietas* relates to the Greek idea of *eusebia* or what we usually call holiness. One's *pietas*, or careful obedience relates to their *religio*. Indeed, we see the basis for the word religion in the Roman idea of *religio*, which was healthy respect or awe for the deity and concern for when *pietas* was violated or dismissed. One unique feature that separates ancient Judaism and early Christianity from the Roman world was in the realm of ethics and morality. One area largely unattended by ancient religions was the realm of morality. Although we typically equate religion and morality today, such would not be the case in the ancient world. Put bluntly, the Roman deities were not concerned with how one lived outside of the four walls of their temple. What one did with one's body was of little concern to Athena, Janus, Artemis, Mars, or any other deity. They were merely concerned with their prayers and sacrifices. One result of this reality is that one did not look to a priest to figure out what was good or evil, right or wrong, good or bad. The one exception to this, of course, was ancient Judaism. Instead, if one wanted moral advice or wisdom, one looked not to priests, but ancient moral philosophers. It was moral philosophy, dating back to at least Aristotle, that was concerned with "the good life," and this inherently included the moral categories of good and evil, right and wrong. Another peculiar feature of early Christianity was that their teachers looked much less like priests and sounded much more like moral philosophers with a way of life for their adherents. If you met Paul in the ancient world, you might think of him as a traveling philosopher, rather than a religious functionary. Early Christianity, of course, looked very dissimilar to ancient religions in this regard and bore a similarity to ancient Judaism from which it was formed and emerged.

CHAPTER THIRTY-THREE

SAUL AND BARNABAS APOSTLES

From Antioch

On the long trek back from Jerusalem, there were four travelers—John Mark, Titus, Saul, and Barnabas who remarked at length about how bold Saul was in his comments.

"I myself could not have pressed the matter that hard, though I think you have the better of the argument. If Gentiles are to be full and equal partners in Christ and even leaders in the movement, and if as you say what has saved them is not being integrated into Judaism, but into this new people, Jew and Gentile united through faith in Jesus the Savior of all, united in a new covenant, then there is a sense in which all of us had to become new creatures in Christ, and had to let the old pass away. Or as Jesus once said we all must be born again, born from above, whatever our past. But of course much of the ethical substance of Torah was reaffirmed by Jesus—no adultery, no murder, no idolatry, and so on."

"True," replied Paul, "but the reason we keep such commandments is because they have been carried over into the new covenant. They are part of what I would call the Law or Instructions of Christ, rather than the Law of Moses. Of course this overlap between the ethical teaching of Torah and that of Jesus will confuse many because they assume that the Mosaic covenant is perpetual, instead of an interim arrangement until the new covenant could be established by the death of Jesus.

"Clearly, the Pharisaic followers of Christ have not yet seen the full implications of the Good News of Jesus, and it was not clear to me that Jacob fully understood either, but he was thinking about it and working on it, and could not deny the genuine Christian faith of Titus. As for Peter, he seemed to agree. I myself was amazed how much he had aged since I last saw him eleven years ago. Jacob looked older of course too, but not like Peter. What has Peter been doing this last decade?"

"From what I hear," replied Barnabas, "he has been gradually evangelizing Jews up and down the coast of Judea, and perhaps you heard that he and John went and confirmed the evangelistic work of Philip in Samaria, laid hands on the Samaritans and they received the Holy Spirit."

"One would have thought that would have been enough to convince the Jerusalem church that this movement was not going to simply be another sect of Judaism."

"Yes, I see your point, but remember, the Samaritans were not Gentiles, even Judeans who dislike the Samaritans, still think they were at least partially Jewish to begin with."

"I suppose," said Saul. "So what happens when we get back to Antioch?"

"Well, we give a full report, and tell the household meetings there that they should carry on meeting together as Jew and Gentile united in Christ."

"Yes . . . but I think God has in mind that we take the message on the road in the Greco-Roman world."

"Where would you go?" asked Barnabas.

"I don't know, make a suggestion."

"We could go to my home country—Cyprus. There are lots of Jews and Greeks and Romans there."

"OK, and after that?"

"You would go further?'

"Yes. Jesus told me take the message to the nations and their kings. We can't just stop in Cyprus."

John Mark interrupted and said, "Uncle Barnabas I had thought we might just be going to Cyprus after Antioch and I could see our kin."

"Well, yes my boy, we can do some of that, but it's not the main purpose of our work. We are to be evangelists for Christ, and we need your enthusiasm and willingness to work to help us along."

Mark was silent after that, and Saul was pondering already if it was a mistake to bring along John Mark, but he said nothing. As for Titus he was simply trudging along, glad the intense meeting in Jerusalem was behind him. He shuddered when the Pharisaic followers of Jesus kept insisting he must be circumcised. Thankfully, that moment passed.

The band of four had traveled by land all the way to Joppa, and from there had taken passage on a small boat heading for Antioch. The waves were a bit whipped by the wind, and John Mark, having never sailed before, got seasick and threw up over the bow of the ship, after which he felt better. Barnabas loved his nephew and had great hopes for him as a sharer of the Gospel. After all, he had been there the very night Jesus was betrayed and had seen what had happened.[1] Neither he himself, nor Saul, nor Titus could claim to be an eyewitness of Jesus.

When they arrived back in Antioch, there was much celebration that the Jerusalem church had endorsed the mission to the Gentiles, and called Paul an apostle for the Gentiles. They held a joint open area meeting just outside the city walls, since it was spring and the weather was good, a meeting full of joyful singing and fasting for the day, and during that meeting Simeon called Niger, a prophet stood up in the meeting, and full of the Spirit, said "The Lord says, set aside for me Barnabas and Saul for the work to which I have called them." And they laid hands on the two men and pledged funds and support for their missionary trip to Cyprus. They had become "apostles," sent ones of the Antioch church, the first church to accept and endorse the label *christianoi*. John Mark was eager to go on this trip, but Titus decided he would stay in Antioch, and study the Scriptures while they were gone. Little did he know they would be away for the rest of the year, and then some.[2] It was to be on Cyprus where Saul would well and truly take the lead in evangelism, and even speak boldly before the governor, Sergius Paulus, who when he asked Saul what his Greek or Latin name was, Saul replied without hesitation that Paulus was his Roman name, and the Greeks called him Paulos.[3] He told the governor he was a Roman citizen, and so impressed was the governor, that he had given a letter of reference to Saul so he could go and share his message openly in the town where Sergius Paulus' family lived—Pisidian Antioch at the border of the Galatian province. This opened a door in Galatia and Paul walked boldly through it, going on to other Galatian cities—Iconium, Lystra, and even on to Derbe.

1. See Mark 14:51–52.

2. The story of the so-called first missionary journey of Paul is told quite vividly by Luke in Acts 13–14, and we will not repeat it here.

3. Notice that the name change does not show up in Acts before Saul speaks to Sergius Paulus—Acts 13:9.

John Mark, however, had gotten homesick, and left the mission once it got to the mainland in Perge.

The Sergius Paulus inscription, now in the museum at Pisidian Antioch.

CHAPTER THIRTY-FOUR

RETURN TO ANTIOCH

When Saul returned to Antioch, now insisting on being called Paul since he was well and truly the missionary to the Gentiles, he was met by Peter, who had been visiting the Christ-followers there for some weeks, and even happily dining in Gentile houses without worrying about finding a mikveh thereafter. Paul rejoiced to see this as it meant, Paul thought, that Peter had come fully around to Paul's view of the nature of the Gospel.

But it was not two days after Paul arrived back in Antioch that the "Judaizers" showed up, having been sent by Jacob to see what was happening at Antioch. The Judaizers were the Pharisaic Jewish Christians still opposed to a Gospel that didn't require all parties to keep the full Mosaic law and covenant. And these men thought they had the endorsement of Jacob to sort things out in Antioch and elsewhere, when in fact, Jacob had asked only for a fact-finding mission on their part.

They began by tracking down Peter and reading him the riot act for eating Gentile food with Gentiles, and they claimed they had the backing from Jacob, which was not quite true. So Peter, to appease these men, withdrew from table fellowship with Gentiles, much to the dismay of not only the Gentiles, but also Paul! Then they accosted Barnabas himself, a man twice their age and with twice as much wisdom and experience, and when they kept insisting this was Jacob's will, he too withdrew from Antioch table fellowship with Gentiles.

These two unexpected events set Paul into a furor. Deeply hurt, especially by Barnabas' reactionary behavior, he chose to confront Peter—in a household meeting. He accused him to his face, publicly shaming him:

RETURN TO ANTIOCH

"You are a Jew, yet you live like a Gentile and not like a Jew. How is it, then, that you force Gentiles to follow Jewish customs?

"We who are Jews by birth and not sinful Gentiles know that a person is not set right by the works of the law, but by the faithfulness of Jesus Christ. So we, too, have put our faith in Christ Jesus that we may be set right by the faithfulness of Christ and not by the works of the law, because by the works of the law no one will be justified.

"But if, in seeking to be justified in Christ, we Jews find ourselves also among the sinners, doesn't that mean that Christ promotes sin? Absolutely not! If I rebuild what I destroyed, then I really would be a lawbreaker.

"For through the law I died to the law so that I might live for God. I have been crucified with Christ and I no longer live, but Christ lives in me. The life I now live in the body, I live by faith in the Son of God, who loved me and gave himself for me. I do not set aside the grace of God, for if righteousness could be gained through the law, Christ died for nothing!"[1]

Paul threw down the gauntlet, and Peter had no response. The polemic didn't convince him to go back to eating with Gentiles on that day. In fact, all he said was "I had better go talk to Jacob, and see what his will really is in these matter. After all, he is Jesus' brother." And thus he left Antioch with both regret and guilt troubling him. When he later found out that the Judaizers had gone well beyond what Jacob had asked them to do, he was furious, and vowed to make amends when he had time and opportunity to do so.[2]

As for the Judaizers, they also left town quickly, destination unknown. Only much later did Paul learn that they had gone through the Cilician gates and on to the churches he had founded in Galatia, trying to undo what he and Barnabas had worked so hard to accomplish. It was this further interference that prompted Paul to write his earliest letter, a circular letter to the churches in Pisidian Antioch, Iconium, and Lystra.[3]

The matter would not be resolved until the following year with a third meeting in Jerusalem in which Jacob finally sided with Paul, and Peter as well against the Judaizers, only requiring Gentiles to avoid idol temples, idol worship, and the idol feasts which involved both non-Kosher food and also immorality, not to mention that a false god was said to be the host and present at such a meal. Paul promised Jacob that he would insist on

---

1. Gal 2:14–21.
2. Which I suggest is what we see in his speech in Acts 15.
3. The letter to the Galatians.

the essence of the decree in his churches, and rapprochement had at least partially been restored between the more Gentile and the more Jewish part of the Jesus movement.[4]

Finally, Paul went back to Barnabas, hoping to restore their relationship. Barnabas suggested they could go back to Cyprus, bringing John Mark along and giving him a second chance. Paul thought that a bad idea, and so they sadly parted ways, Barnabas to return to Cyprus with Mark, Paul instead to go overland back to Galatia this time taking with him Silas, to whom the Decree of Jacob had been given and the task to read it out in the newly minted, mostly Gentile churches of Paul. They were to become fast friends, partners in ministry, and along the way they recruited Timothy in Lystra, who was to become like a son to Paul, who had no offspring. With the writing of the letter to the Galatians, followed by the so-called second missionary journey of Paul, the "hidden years" of the apostle to the Gentiles were over. He was now to become the most visible advocate of Christ and Him crucified and risen from Antioch to Asia Minor to Greece, and ultimately to Rome. But the story of Paul does not begin with conversion, followed immediately by successful missionary journeys. It begins with at least fourteen years of trial and error, fear and terror, personal tragedy and beatings. Later Paul would eloquently sum all of this by saying the following to his Corinthian converts:

"Therefore, since through God's mercy we have this ministry, we do not lose heart. Rather, we have renounced secret and shameful ways; we do not use deception, nor do we distort the word of God. On the contrary, by setting forth the truth plainly we commend ourselves to everyone's conscience in the sight of God. And even if our gospel is veiled, it is veiled to those who are perishing. The god of this age has blinded the minds of unbelievers, so that they cannot see the light of the gospel that displays the glory of Christ, who is the image of God. For what we preach is not ourselves, but Jesus Christ as Lord, and ourselves as your servants for Jesus' sake. For God, who said, 'Let light shine out of darkness,' made his light shine in our hearts to give us the light of the knowledge of God's glory displayed in the face of Christ.

"But we have this treasure in jars of clay to show that this all-surpassing power is from God and not from us. We are hard pressed on every side, but not crushed; perplexed, but not in despair; persecuted, but not

---

4. Cf. Acts 15 and the decree there to Paul's insistence in 1 Cor 8–10 that his converts stay awayfrom idols and idol feasts.

abandoned; struck down, but not destroyed. We always carry around in our body the death of Jesus, so that the life of Jesus may also be revealed in our body. For we who are alive are always being given over to death for Jesus' sake, so that his life may also be revealed in our mortal body. So then, death is at work in us, but life is at work in you.

"It is written: 'I believed; therefore I have spoken.' Since we have that same spirit of faith, we also believe and therefore speak, because we know that the one who raised the Lord Jesus from the dead will also raise us with Jesus and present us with you to himself. All this is for your benefit, so that the grace that is reaching more and more people may cause thanksgiving to overflow to the glory of God.

"Therefore we do not lose heart. Though outwardly we are wasting away, yet inwardly we are being renewed day by day. For our light and momentary troubles are achieving for us an eternal glory that far outweighs them all. So we fix our eyes not on what is seen, but on what is unseen, since what is seen is temporary, but what is unseen is eternal" (2 Cor 4).

THE END

POSTSCRIPT

THE STORY OF THE HIDDEN YEARS OF SAUL/PAUL IS A TUMULTUOUS STORY. It was a full fourteen years after his conversion, if not more, before he actually had converts to write about or to, and some measure of success in fulfilling his commission. There had been many trials and tragedies along the way before the light of the good news brought chiefly by Paul broke through the clouds of unknowing in the Greco-Roman world. No one could have known in the mid-first century AD that Paul and his gospel would not merely change the Jesus movement, it would quite literally change the world, and would continue to do so unto this very day.

It is important in an age of instant everything to realize that many important things done for the cause of Christ do not result in instant converts, success, fame, and the various tokens the modern world calls significant achievement. Paul was no overnight sensation or success. My hope is that this historically-based novella will put a damper on some of the wrong sorts of triumphalism one often hears proclaimed in the church these days, where some have even had the temerity to suggest a "name it and claim it" approach to faith, and to suggest that failure or tragedy is always a result of lack of faith. It would be better if we went back to the motto of one of the first Quaker settlers in the New World, William Penn who said: "no pain, no palm, no thorns no throne, no gall, no glory, no cross, no crown." If it was ever thus for Jesus and Paul, why should we expect it to be any different for us? The question is—will we, like Jesus and Paul, through all our trials and tribulations maintain that unwavering faith and unconquerable spirit referred to in 2 Cor 4?

BIBLIOGRAPHY

Bowersock, G. W. *Roman Arabia*. Cambridge: Harvard University Press, 1983.
Bowman, Alan, et al., eds. *The Cambridge Ancient History, Vol 10: The Augustan Empire: 43 B. C.-A. D. 69*. 2nd ed. New York: Cambridge University Press, 1996.
Bryce, Trevor. *Ancient Syria: A Three Thousand Year History*. New York: Oxford University Press, 2014.
Cohick, Lynn. "Women, Children, and Families in the Greco-Roman World." In *The World of the New Testament*, edited by Joel B. Green and Lee Martin McDonald, 179–87. Grand Rapids: Baker, 2013.
Coleman, Kathleen M. "Public Entertainments." In *The Oxford Handbook of Social Relations in the Roman World*, edited by Michael Peachin, 335–58. New York: Oxford University Press, 2011.
Collins, John J. "Death and Afterlife." In *The Eerdmans Dictionary of Early Judaism*, edited by John J. Collins and Daniel C. Harlow, 524–26. Grand Rapids: Eerdmans, 2010.
Dixon, Suzanne. *The Roman Family*. Baltimore: Johns Hopkins University Press, 1992.
Ferguson, Everett. *Backgrounds of Early Christianity*. Grand Rapids: Eerdmans, 2003.
Galinsky, Karl. *Augustan Culture*. Princeton: Princeton University Press, 1996.
Garnsey, Peter and Saller, Richard. *The Roman Empire: Economy Society, and Culture*. Berkeley: University of California Press, 1987.
Grabbe, Lester L. *Judaism from Cyrus to Hadrian Vol 2: The Roman Period*. Minneapolis: Fortress, 1992.
Hachili, Rachel. "Burial Practices." In *The Eerdmans Dictionary of Early Judaism*, edited by John J. Collins and Daniel C. Harlow, 448–52. Grand Rapids: Eerdmans, 2003.
Harrill, J. Albert. "Paul and Slavery." In *Paul in the Greco-Roman World: A Handbook*, edited by J. Paul Sampley, 575–607. Harrisburg: Trinity, 2003.
Harris, W. V. "Child-Exposure in the Roman Empire." *JRS* 84 (1994) 1–22.
Hermann-Otto, Elisabeth. "Slaves and Freedmen." In *The Cambridge Companion to Ancient Rome*, edited by Paul Erdkamp, 60–76. New York: Cambridge University Press, 2013.
Hornblower, Simon, and Antony Spawforth, eds. *The Oxford Classical Dictionary*. New York: Oxford University Press, 1999.
Instone-Brewer, David. "Marriage and Divorce." In *The Eerdmans Dictionary of Second Temple Judaism*, edited by John J. Collins and Daniel C. Harlow, 916–17. Grand Rapids: Eerdmans, 2010.
Isaac, Benjamin. *The Near East Under Roman Rule: Selected Papers*. Leiden: Brill, 1998.
Joshel, Sandra. *Slavery in the Roman World*. New York: Cambridge University Press, 2010.

BIBLIOGRAPHY

Judge, E. A. *Social Distinctives of the Christians in the First Century.* Peabody, MA: Hendrickson, 2008.

Keener, Craig. *Acts: An Exegetical Commentary.* Grand Rapids: Baker, 2012.

Kehoe, Dennis P. "Law and Social Formation in the Roman Empire." In *The Oxford Handbook of Social Relations in the Roman World*, edited by Michael Peachin, 144-66. New York: Oxford University Press, 2011.

Laes, Christian. *Children in the Roman Empire: Outsiders Within.* New York: Cambridge University Press, 2011.

Matthews, Victor. "Family, Children, and Inheritance in the Biblical World." In *Behind the Scenes of the Old Testament: Cultural, Social, and Historical Contexts*, edited by Jonathan S. Greer et al., 403-10. Grand Rapids: Baker, 2018.

Millar, Fergus. *The Roman Near East: 31 BC-AD 337.* Cambridge: Harvard University Press, 1993.

Neils, Jennifer. "Women in Rome." In *The Oxford Encyclopedia of Ancient Greece and Rome*, edited by Michael Gagarin et al., 7:250-51. New York: Oxford University Press, 2010.

Meeks, Wayne. *The First Urban Christians.* New Haven, CT: Yale University Press, 2003.

Rawson, Beryl. "Marriages, Families, Households." In *The Cambridge Companion to Ancient Rome*, edited by Paul Erdkamp, 93-109. New York: Cambridge University Press, 2013.

Reiss, Werner. "The Roman Bandit (Latro) as Criminal and Outsider." In *The Oxford Handbook of Social Relations in the Roman World*, edited by Michael Peachin, 693-714. New York: Oxford University Press, 2011.

Sanders, E. P. *Paul and Palestinian Judaism.* Philadelphia: Fortress, 1977.

Scott, James M., ed. *Exile: A Conversation with N. T. Wright.* Downers Grove, IL: InterVarsity, 2017.

Tate, Joshua C. "Christianity and the Legal Status of Abandoned Children in the Later Roman Empire." *Journal of Law and Religion* 24 (2008) 123-41.

Treggiari, Susan. "Social Status and Social Legislation." In *The Cambridge Ancient History, Vol 10*, edited by Alan Bowman et al., 873-904. New York: Cambridge University Press, 1996.

Yarbrough, O. Larry. "Paul, Marriage, and Divorce." In *Paul in the Greco-Roman World: A Handbook*, edited by. J. Paul Sampley, 404-28. Harrisburg: Trinity, 2003.

Wansink, Craig. "Roman Law and Legal System." *In The Dictionary of New Testament Background*, edited by Craig A. Evans and Stanley J. Porter, 986-87. Downers Grove, IL: InterVarsity, 2000.

Weiss, Zeiv. "Theatres, Hippodromes, Amphitheaters, and Perfomances." in *The Oxford Handbook of Jewish Daily Life in Roman Palestine*, edited by Catherine Hezser, 623-40. New York: Oxford University Press, 2010.

Witherington, Ben, III. *Conflict and Community in Corinth: A Socio-Rhetorical Commentary on 1 and 2 Corinthians.* Grand Rapids: Eerdmans, 1995.

———. *The Acts of the Apostles: A Socio-Rhetorical Commentary.* Grand Rapids: Eerdmans, 1998.

———. *Isaiah Old and New.* Minneapolis: Fortress, 2017.

Wright, N. T. *The New Testament and the People of God.* Christian Origins and the Question of God, vol. 1. Minneapolis: Fortress, 1992.

www.ingramcontent.com/pod-product-compliance
Lightning Source LLC
Chambersburg PA
CBHW051744230426
43670CB00012B/2160